CULTURAL GENOCIDE

Genocide, Political Violence, Human Rights Series

Edited by Alexander Laban Hinton, Stephen Eric Bronner, and Nela Navarro

Lawrence Davidson, *Cultural Genocide*

Alexander Laban Hinton, ed., *Transitional Justice: Global Mechanisms and Local Realities after Genocide and Mass Violence*

Irina Silber, *Everyday Revolutionaries: Gender, Violence, and Disillusionment in Postwar El Salvador*

Samuel Totten and Rafiki Ubaldo, eds., *We Cannot Forget: Interviews with Survivors of the 1994 Genocide in Rwanda*

Ronnie Yimsut, *Facing the Khmer Rouge: A Cambodian Journey*

CULTURAL GENOCIDE

LAWRENCE DAVIDSON

RUTGERS UNIVERSITY PRESS
NEW BRUNSWICK, NEW JERSEY, AND LONDON

Library of Congress Cataloging-in-Publication Data

Davidson, Lawrence, 1945–
    Cultural genocide / Lawrence Davidson.
        p. cm — (Genocide, political violence, human rights series)
    Includes bibliographical references and index.
    ISBN 978-0-8135-5243-9 (hardcover : alk. paper) —
ISBN 978-0-8135-5349-8 (pbk. : alk. paper)— ISBN 978-0-8135-5344-3
(e-book)
    1. Ethnic conflict.   2. Persecution—Social aspects.   3. Assimilation
(Sociology)   4. Indians, Treatment of—North America—History.
5. Jews—Russia—Social conditions—19th century.   6. Palestinian Arabs—
Israel—Social conditions—20th century.   7. Tibet Autonomous Region
(China)—Social conditions.   I. Title.
    HM1121.D375   2012
    305.8009—dc23

                                                            2011023488

A British Cataloging-in-Publication record for this book is available from the
British Library.

Visit our Web site: http://rutgerspress.rutgers.edu

Manufactured in the United States of America

*For all the victims of cultural genocide,
whose destruction constitutes the slow extinction
of human variety. For all the victims of idolatry
masquerading as ideologies and religions.*

*This book is also dedicated to Frances Davidson and Zelda Nefsky,
who survived the anti-Semitism of their youth
to go on and live productive and happy lives.*

*And special thanks go to David Metter, among the best of my former
students. His comments on the text proved most helpful.*

CONTENTS

CULTURAL GENOCIDE

1

THEORETICAL
FOUNDATIONS

What are the circumstances by which large proportions of a community, be it a neighborhood or a nation, come to see others as so dangerous that they will attack them with genocidal intent? How is it that people who have never met or even seen anyone of a specified different group can be brought to hate those individuals? Why is it that we can be brought to see other people's values as not only strange but also polluting? Historically, these situations have occurred repeatedly and continue to manifest themselves today. There is no reason to believe that they are not also waiting in our future. This chapter will offer a theoretical context for answering these questions. In doing so, it will lay the basis for an understanding of another, under-recognized and under-studied, phenomenon: cultural genocide.

When we speak of cultural genocide we are not referring to the global nature of the fast-food industry, the homogenizing of clothing styles along Western lines, or the apparent persistent desire of millions of people of non-European backgrounds to migrate to the United States or the European Union. Rather we are interested in purposeful destructive targeting of out-group cultures so as to destroy or weaken them in the process of conquest or domination.

Much of this book will look at case studies of such occurrences. Cultural genocide, too, has long been with us and continues into the present. However, unlike its more recognized and bloodier counterpart, physical genocide, it is not yet illegal under international law. The book will close with an effort to answer the question of why this is so. But first things first. How is it that communities can be brought to acquiesce in the cultural genocide of others? The answer has a lot to do with a phenomenon this author has called natural localness.

NATURAL LOCALNESS

The modern assumption is that we live in a global age. This proposition was most famously stated by Marshall McLuhan in a series of books and articles written in the early 1960s. Using an anatomical metaphor, McLuhan tells us in the introduction to *Understanding Media* that "after more than a century of electric [*sic*] technology, we have extended our central nervous system in a global embrace" (McLuhan 1964, 3). To use a more modern vernacular, McLuhan is asserting that the whole world is "wired" and that makes us all citizens of a "global village" within which communication "time has ceased" and "space has vanished." This, in turn, allows us to exchange information across the planet in the same fashion and speed as we would across town (McLuhan 1967, 63). There is no doubt that this wiring process is proceeding, though it certainly has not yet covered the entire planet. The World Wide Web represents a growing link to a world of information.

However, the conclusion that McLuhan draws from this ongoing process is questionable. There is a difference between the technology of communication and the extent and nature of its use. There is a difference between the existence of the World Wide Web and the purpose to which it is put by a majority of its users. Both usage and content often remain local in nature. For instance, according to a recent Stanford University study, most Americans with access to the Web are using it to e-mail friends and to shop ("The Internet Study: More Detail" 2000). That is, the Web serves them as an expedited mail and catalog service. These pursuits suggest that the dominant popular interest of even the most global of technologies is provincial and personal.

This calls into serious doubt the assumption that globalism, at least as it pertains to the daily life of ordinary people, has qualitatively broadened interests or perspectives. More likely, today as in the past, the natural preference of most human beings is to orient their lives locally. Suggestive evidence for this orientation comes from a recent study tracking cell phone use for six months among one hundred thousand randomly selected non-Americans. The study revealed that human movement has "a high degree of temporal and spatial regularity, each individual being characterized by a time-independent characteristic travel distance and a significant probability to return to a few frequented locations." As a consequence, daily travel for most people seems to take place within a roughly twenty-mile radius (Gonzalez, Hidalgo, and Barabasi 2008, 779).

There is also the fact that on a day-to-day basis, it is our immediate environment that is most important to all of us. That is to say, important knowledge is knowledge relative to us and our environment. The local environment supplies the vast majority of us with our arena of work and sustenance, and is where we usually find our immediate family circle, friends, and peer groups. It is also where our everyday problem solving takes place. To "get by," we need information that allows for this level of problem solving, and it is only to be found locally. For instance, what matters to most of us on a daily basis is local highway traffic patterns to and from work and school, and not the estimated times of arrival and departure in and out of the regional airport. On occasion the latter might concern us, but for most it is only an extraordinary, not ordinary, occurrence.

Beyond problem solving, we are interested in the gossip and coming and going of our locale just because it is local and connected to us. Some of us have close relatives and friends abroad and, in a virtual way, their locale is sometimes integrated with ours, but this also is an exceptional situation. On the whole, rather than following events further off, we are interested in town or neighborhood news: weddings, restaurant and movie reviews, obituaries, local instances of crime, and department store sales. This priority of the local is not diminished by the advances in communication technology that are said to "epitomize the 'end of geography' and the 'death of distance' " (Wittkopf and McCormack 1999, xi).

This situation lends itself to a Darwinian analysis. We know that in the course of its evolution, the human mind became "equipped with faculties to master the local environment and outwit denizens" (Pinker 1997, 352). We all pay particular attention to our local arena because it supplies us with knowledge necessary to make useful and usually successful predictions, secure sustenance, and avoid danger. In other words, a concentration on the local environment has survival value. There are nature and nurture components to this. On the one hand, there are biological, hard-wired imperatives that make us group-oriented, suspicious of the unknown, and sensitive to fear and danger. This plays out most readily in the territorial range in which we dwell. On the other hand, how we manifest these imperatives is a function of what we learn from our personal experiences, which, in turn, takes place within a cultural context and is dependent on the quality of information available to us. Within our immediate daily environment, we can be responsible for gathering the necessary information. Beyond the horizon, however, the issue of information and its reliability becomes problematic.

Natural localness is not just a phenomenon experienced by the individual. It is also a group orientation. Culture is a bounded paradigm that flows from the customs and traditions of local and regional venues. Since early modern times, local and regional areas have politically coalesced into nation-states, which amalgamate and manipulate local customs and traditions. Local culture (customized so as to be compatible with national culture) defines not only acceptable behaviors but to a large extent the very parameters of thought. That is, culture establishes perceptual limits for the average person's outlook. It makes no difference that the shape of all cultural paradigms as they apply to the concept of nationhood are artificial and "imagined," as Benedict Anderson puts it (Anderson 1991, 6). A culture's prevailing paradigm is so natural to its adherents that it operates unconsciously. The process of maintaining culture prioritizes "coherence" and "difference from that which is outside." In this way, "borders become central to understanding concepts and practices such as identity, belonging and culture" (Sajed n.d.). Thus it would seem that, even in this day and age of international travel, satellite dishes, and economic globalization, we are still, as individuals and communities, locally oriented. If you will, the "global village" is significantly segregated into self-centered neighborhoods.

Although there are good reasons why most of us are locally oriented, natural localness has its shortcomings. "Tuning out the rest of the globe" (Granitsas 2005) and concentrating on one's locality means that most of us live largely in ignorance about what is going on beyond the proverbial next hill. This ignorance can reinforce evolution-bred emotions of exclusiveness that are reflected in a suspicion and dislike of outsiders. As the cognitive psychologist Keith Oatley has written, "Our [evolutionary] forebears had a tendency to treat members of out-groups . . . with contempt and sometimes murderous aggression" (Oatley 2004, 29). Even in a country as

diverse as the United States, localness prevails among the various
ethnic groups that are potentially phobic toward each other in proportion to their ignorance of one another. The situation also results
in periodic, almost cyclical outbursts against "illegal" aliens (Ngai
2004). In this environment, accurate information about the lifestyle
and intentions of our neighbors is important to the maintenance of
intergroup peace. Yet, as we will see, most often we do not have such
information, and so the proclivity for negative feelings is subject to
manipulation by the media, politicians, religious authorities, and
others.

GETTING OUR PICTURE OF THE OUTSIDE WORLD

How do the naturally local majority obtain their picture of the
outside world and its inhabitants? The process was insightfully
described by Walter Lippman in his book *Public Opinion*, first
published in 1922 (here we are using the 1997 edition). In this work
he described the perceptions most people have of the world beyond
their locale in terms of indirectly acquired stereotypes. An important aspect of his critique was the assertion that the farther from
home we look, the more dependent we are on limited and often
distorted information coming from sources we know little about.
This information underpins the "pictures in our heads," as Lippman
characterized them, that flesh out the superficial views we hold of
nonlocal events and peoples and their possible impact on our lives.
Here is how Lippman explained our predicament: "Each of us lives
and works on a small part of the earth's surface, moves in a small
circle. . . . Inevitably our opinions cover a bigger space, a longer
reach of time, a greater number of things, than we can directly
observe. They have, therefore, to be pieced together out of what
others have reported and what we can imagine" (Lippman 1997, 53).

It is in times of high tension involving those not of our community that we become most aware of our ignorance on matters that range beyond our local environment. To compensate for that ignorance, we automatically place the situation within a culturally prescribed context. This is a sort of general background sensibility that is usually driven by stereotypes. We simultaneously turn to others of our group who, it is assumed, know what is going on abroad. The primary source that brings us these "experts"—government officials, pundits, academics, and sometimes religious officials—is the news media in all its forms. However, as Lippman tells us, "news and truth are not the same thing" (Lippman 1997, 226). One of the reasons for the divergence is the fact that the news is filtered through the minds of those "experts in the know" and their media facilitators. And as the legal theorist Richard Posner tells us, these "experts constitute a distinct class in society, with values and perspectives that differ systematically from those of 'ordinary' people" (Posner 2003, 206). Thus, going back to Lippman, we can assume that the guidance offered by the "experts" is "in some vital measure constructed out of [their] own stereotypes . . . and by the urgency of [their] own interest" (Lippman 1997, 227).

In other words, those offering authoritative guidance, being as much prisoners of stereotypes as those listening to them, will have their own "pictures in their heads," influenced by their own vested interests. Those vested interests are often shaped by their personal ideological, religious, and political affiliations, as well as the media outlets that assist them in spreading their message. This inevitably leads them to present biased, or "stylized," pictures of events. It makes little difference if some or even most of these informants truly believe that their positions reflect reality. Consciously or unconsciously, they are in the business of stylizing the nonlocal world.

This scenario fits well with the position taken by Noam Chomsky and Edward Herman in their book *Manufacturing Consent*. Here they put forth a "propaganda model" to describe mass media that "filter" the news and rely on "information provided by the government, business, and 'experts' funded and approved by these sources and agents of power" (Chomsky and Herman 1988, 2). It is such conditions that can result, in the words of Janice J. Terry, in a "near unanimity of view" on almost all issues, including those having to do with outsiders, as well as a tendency for the media to approach the news in a way that is "prone to support the established powerful elite" (Terry 2005, 22ff.). Such are "the grim realities of modern American journalism," as William Rivers Pitt puts it, that makes the old maxim "buyer beware" now apply to the news (Pitt 2007).

Factoring in Hardwired Emotions

A real and serious danger with this process of stylization is that it can tap into hardwired predispositions, with the most destructive consequences. Although we humans might pride ourselves as being individuals with "free will," we are in fact carriers of an array of emotions shaped by seventy million years of mammalian evolution. According to the cognitive psychologist Keith Oatley, one consequence of this primordial fact is that "emotions can drive thoughts . . . in an involuntary way" and "act as a goad" to action (Oatley 2004, 11–12).

According to Oatley, the array of genetically rooted predispositions that strongly influence everyday behavior are expressed in three culturally constructed categories. The first is assertiveness, which reflects a pursuit of status and power and also leads to a natural bias for those with shared interests. If one doubts the ubiquitous power of such emotion, just consider that the theme of conflict arising over such pursuits historically makes up the second largest topic in human literature. The next category is attachment to others, which reflects the pursuit of security against danger. It probably overlaps with the third category, affiliation, which reflects the pursuit of love, friendship, and cooperation. Historically, the most common historical theme in human literature is love (Oatley 2004, 2, 90–91).

The issue of stylization comes into this through the fact that emotions reflecting these primordial needs and drives can be consciously harnessed through the use of "emotives" or forms of speech and action that create "emotional regimes" or paradigms. Emotives most often help reinforce love of one's group, be it ethnic, religious, or national. They also promote "the contempt and hatred" that one feels for enemies. Oatley is of the opinion that "in America today . . . emotives have been used to induce hostility to 'terrorism'" without recourse to analysis or accurate examination of context. Laws too can sometimes take on the character of codified emotives (Oatley 2004, 17). There is no reason, of course, why emotives cannot be used to promote universal friendship and cooperation, which is what Jesus allegedly tried to do. It does not seem to have worked, even among Christians.

The connection between emotion and stylization makes the next step easier. If this process of stylization, applied to events beyond one's small part of the earth's surface, is done with consistency across the media spectrum and over a sufficiently long time, it will produce generally similar pictures in the heads of local, regional, and even national populations. What results is a "thought collective." This term was originally used by Ludwik Fleck to describe the socially determined collective approach to scientific research, but it has much wider application. Thought collectives are artificially created, community-wide points of view, the most prevalent example of which is the nation-state itself—that universal phenomenon which Benedict Anderson calls "striking . . . imaginings of fraternity"

(Anderson 1991, 203). Thought collectives take on added strength from the fact that most people shape their opinions to coincide with those around them. People want to fit into their community, and sharing outlooks is an important aspect of this bonding. Once the shared perspective is in place, there is a natural tendency to reinforce it by seeking out information that supports it and ignoring or downplaying that which does not. Ultimately, media- and government-manipulated thought collectives can move populations to action on the basis of firmly implanted assumptions, which, in turn, are often based on stereotypes, buzzwords, and unanalyzed assertions. If the implanted assumptions tap into cultural prejudices, the effect can be greatly magnified.

Recognizing the Dangers

The danger stemming from such a state of affairs has been recognized for a very long time. When René Descartes sat down to use reason to discover what could reliably be said to be true he was, in part, reacting against the fact that "many things which, however extravagant and ridiculous to our apprehension, are yet by common consent received and approved" (Descartes 2008, 15). Ernest Gellner, exploring the ramifications of Descartes's position, points out that it is society's young people who are most at risk from cultural nonsense. It is the youth who are routinely acculturated to customary meanings. Gellner sadly notes, "Infancy, youth, and maturation are a kind of original corrupting sin. . . . They expose us to custom and example at a time when we are ill-equipped to resist them, for in our immaturity we know no better and they permeate us" (Gellner 1992, 4). This is not merely an individual problem. It is a community one. Continuing his reflections on Descartes's skepticism about custom and tradition, Gellner laments, "What is disturbing is not that

I am liable to err, but that the shared assumptions of an entire society, built into its way of life and sustained by it, should be deeply
misguided" (Gellner 1992, 2). The evolving interconnectedness of
local, regional, and national communities is in no way a check on
collective error. And, the reality of thought collectives make "shared
assumptions" all the harder to escape. If the history of intergroup
relations is any guide, both Descartes and Gellner are correct.
Gellner goes on to ask, "This being so, how can we trust our own
collective conviction? We know them [the outsiders] to be fools.
Are we ourselves exempt from folly?" (Gellner 1992, 2). The answer
is emphatically no.

Thus, according to Ernest Gellner, Descartes found "culture and
reason antithetical." Culture is questionable, Reason is not. "Doubt
and Reason must jointly purge our minds," wrote Descartes.
Further, he believed that any rational individual could escape the
influence of his or her culture through the application of independent reason. Gellner explains that "Descartes's rationalism is also pro-
foundly individualistic: one can, he [Descartes] claims, construct a
world on foundations that are not only rational but wholly one's
own" (Gellner 1992, 2–3). Unfortunately, as Gellner's example of
impressionable youth suggests, Descartes is being too optimistic. If
his claim is true, thought collectives would not be the problem that
they most certainly are. Indeed, the average citizen is not capable of
what Descartes suggests, and local naturalness has a lot to do with
this fact.

This deficiency is suggested by recent research on critical thinking.
Daniel T. Willingham, a professor of psychology at the University of
Virginia, has looked at much of this research. He has come to the
conclusion that critical thinking is not a skill that can be taught,
"like riding a bicycle." Willingham points out, "The processes of
thinking are intertwined with the content of thought." That is,

intertwined with what he calls domain knowledge. "Thus, if you remind a student to look at an issue from multiple perspectives often enough, he will learn that he ought to do so, but if he doesn't know much about the issue, he *can't* think about it from multiple perspectives." What are the ramifications of the fact that critical thinking is dependent on domain knowledge? One consequence is that you must have "adequate content knowledge" to make critical judgments (Willingham 2007, 8–19). But adequate domain or content knowledge is just what the vast majority of people do not have about nonlocal events. Superficial knowledge, such as that received from "sound bites or brief one-sided stories" simply do not supply sufficient, relatively objective, background information. When we are told that there is a threat to our community from an alien source, or when something actually does come over the hill and impinges on our lives, the knowledge we are given by our media and "experts" is almost always insufficient for making an independent and critical judgment, even if it happens to occur to us that such a judgment is called for.

For instance, take the average American's knowledge of such places as contemporary Iraq and Afghanistan. If all you know about these lands is what has been laid out for you by government spokespersons, generalizing on the attacks of September 11, 2001, from al-Qaeda to the Iraqi nation; or by Christian fundamentalist preachers generalizing things even further to the entire religion of Islam; or from national media no longer capable of independent investigative reporting, how do you think critically about what you are told? How do you even come to the conclusion that there is a need to consider alternative points of view? Under normal circumstances, most Americans are indifferent to events in the Middle East and are not going to take the time and the trouble to make a study of that region and its historical relationship with the United States.

They are simply going to accept the pronouncements of governmental and media spokespersons, along with their underlying emotives, as definitive and true. The risk is then high that they will be caught up in a rabid Islamophobia.

The social scientist Arjun Appadurai has described the resulting emotions as "the severe pathologies" embedded in the "sacred ideologies of nationhood" (Appadurai 2006, 1). In other words, the very same conditions that underpin local, regional, and national community life can, under the right circumstances, become the conditions that intensify intercommunity strife. Appadurai feels that, in recent times, globalism has exacerbated this condition, in the sense that globalism has created conditions in which we no longer fight about just territory and resources. We fight because, increasingly, we are taught by our media and government that the world is no longer big enough to hold competing ways of life. This can only happen if we are unalterably bound to a sanctified localness.

Objections to this position have been made by researchers such as John Mueller and Warren Strobel, who deny the power of the so-called "CNN effect." This is the claim that television and the pictures it can bring into every American home can "set the public agenda and policy mood" (Mueller 1999, 55). Pointing to the sectarian warfare that brought horrors to Bosnia in the 1990s, they note that media coverage did not spark any public demand for American intervention. But all this tells us is that the media and government were not portraying Bosnia as a situation relevant to the listeners' local environment. On the other hand, Iraq was presented in just such a way. If information about a foreign situation, or about any outside group, is put forth in a consistent and coordinated fashion, where media and "pundits" and government "experts" all combine to create a persistent presentation that does purport to relate to the audience's lives, they can command the emotions of a majority of that audience. This manipulation of the informational environment can create the fear and anxiety necessary to move a population to back prepackaged policies.

The ways of seeing that are produced by thought collectives therefore limit domain knowledge and narrow the scope of critical discourse. This raises serious questions about the conclusions reached by such investigators as Bruce Berkowitz and James Surowiecki. They have made the claim that Americans are "reluctant to accept 'wisdom' from authority figures" (Berkowitz 1999, 207). In his book entitled *The Wisdom of Crowds*, Surowiecki tells us that "even if most of the people within a group are not especially well-informed or rational, it can still reach a collectively wise decision" (Surowiecki 2005, xiii). It is possible that this could happen some statistically small number of times in nonemotionally charged environments. But it is improbable one would get a wise decision very often. This is because wise decisions arrived at other than in random chance fashion require a certain level of domain knowledge. One can reasonably ask how the crowd can exercise critical judgment when most of its participants are not well informed or even rational? What is much more probable, particularly in those cases where the situation is presented as dangerously relevant to people's local environment, is Pavlovian response patterns based on media-conditioned habits of association.

This conclusion seems to fit with research on how the mind structures knowledge. According to Steven Pinker, the mind uses categories because they allow us to make inferences about items assigned therein. We do not need to know a lot of details about a subject to think we know enough to react to it. All we have to do is know enough to fit it into a category and then infer the rest from the common characteristics of the selected group (Pinker 1997, 307). And where do we get the smattering of detail that allows us to think

we know enough to react? It comes from the media, the government, and their associated "experts." This is obviously a process that
facilitates stereotyping.

In times of crisis, most people bound to such artificially created
worldviews and the emotions that they elicit will find it almost
impossible to think independently about subjects of which they
know little, but to which they have been sensitized by the media. In
a certain sense the thought collective now takes on the characteristics of a kinship circle. The maintenance of cohesion in the face of
outside threats becomes a family affair. As for the minority of skep-
tics and doubters who somehow escape this acculturation process,
most will tend toward silence in the face of community pressure.

The resulting thought collective usually encompasses the political leadership and societal elites as well as the ordinary citizenry.
That is, the heads of governments usually do believe their own
propaganda. After all, the elites are subject to the same acculturation
process and group dynamics as others and are, therefore, in the
words of Michael H. Hunt, "caught up in the web of ideology" that
complements their society's cultural and political paradigms (Hunt
1987, 2). In addition, their uncritical acceptance of their society's
worldview leads them to protect their assumptions from dissension.
In his book *Victims of Groupthink*, Irving L. Janis shows how governing political elites create self-reinforcing decision-making circles
that emphasize the same "glib ideological formulas on which rational
policy makers, like many other people who share their nationalistic
goals, generally rely in order to maintain self-confidence and cognitive mastery over the complexities of international politics" (Janis
1972, 38). In other words, Lippman was correct. National leaders are
no freer of stereotyped pictures of the world than the masses. And
this is so despite the fact that they have available to them a wider
than normal range of information sources. As is the case generally,

they will put a premium on emphasizing attitudes and points of view that affirm group cohesiveness so as to uphold what Earl C. Ravenal calls "our basic strategic categories—the deep cognitive mindsets embedded in our decision making system" (Ravenal 1978, 51). Information and points of view that challenge standing assumptions and group unity in the face of real or imagined adversity will be filtered out or discounted.

In the end, almost everyone will come to share, or at least go along with, the range of debate that the "establishment" finds acceptable. It is in this way that not only local group cohesiveness is achieved but also regional and national unity. Thus it is not necessary for the manipulation of mass behavior to originate in some conspiratorial cabal standing outside of the thought collective. Just about everyone from the national leadership to the media moguls, to the consumers of news and the voting citizens, is on the inside of the prevailing information environment.

CONCLUSION

Natural localness is like the proverbial two-headed coin. On one side of the coin is engraved the conditions that facilitate community. The educator Sheldon Berman, in his book entitled *Children's Social Consciousness and the Development of Social Responsibility*, tells us that "identity and ideology [community traditions] are two aspects of the same process." And, contra Gellner, he goes on to say that "identification with ideology helps define . . . something to which one can commit oneself. . . . We have a deep human need for a way of organizing both our personal and our own social reality into a larger whole that can give us meaning and direction" (Berman 1997, 63). The human need to identify and draw meaning using traditions is most often satisfied in a locally rooted upbringing. The positive aspects of this form of localism are appealingly laid out in the essays of Wendell Berry (Berry 1990). Over time, however, the local community has slotted itself into larger regional and national groupings. Where this is done successfully, most residents develop loyalties to these greater entities. But this is most likely because these entities successfully subsume our local environment and its traditions. The fact is that natural localness and its customary ways are a necessary part of a stable human existence. The culture they produce is the "glue that holds a group together" (Ater 1998).

It is just because it serves as a basis for community identity that localness must be an inherently bounded state. As such, the other side of the coin that is natural localness is full of potential pitfalls. It is on that side that we find enumerated the consequences of our inherently self-referencing mind-set. These consequences produce a range of outlooks on what is outside the local or community environment that go from intergroup indifference (that is, a basic lack of empathy for the suffering of people beyond the community) to serious intergroup friction, where fear and hatred are the emotions at work.

As a consequence, history is replete with intergroup conflict. Since 1945 and the end of World War II, the world has experienced at least 104 major conflicts that warrant the title of wars. That is a rate of more than two wars a year following on the worldwide conflagration that ended with the use of atomic weapons. What is peculiar about many of these contemporary conflicts is that the informational environments, emotives, and thought collectives that spurred them on did more than just demonize an enemy. They went further to demonize whole cultures and civilizations. In his largely misunderstood book, *The Clash of Civilizations and the Remaking of World Order*, Samuel Huntington argues that such efforts are futile. He tells us that "a multicultural world is unavoidable because global

empire is impossible. . . . The security of the world requires acceptance of global multiculturality" (Huntington 1996, 318). But the
world's media experts and ideologically driven information environments goad us on to take a different path. It is a path down which
the "glue that holds a group together" can metastasize into war and
genocide.

The theoretical considerations put forth in this opening chapter
are designed to help explain why, in our modern world, this path is
repeatedly taken. That is, how the phenomena of war, genocide,
intergroup slaughter, imperial domination, and all such horrors
become possible. In this interpretation, the hardwired emotions
explained by Oatley express themselves, in the case of the vast
majority, within an atmosphere of natural localness. Natural localness in turn limits what Willingham characterizes as domain knowledge. That is, it restricts the range of knowledge necessary to think
critically about situations beyond our local sphere. Because of this,
we have to rely on others, so-called experts presented to us by the
media, the government, and other public sources, to fill the void of
ignorance. We have been taught to accept these sources as reliable
and credible, but we really have no way of testing if their information is truthful. In fact, as Lippman asserts, these sources often have
their own agendas and therefore "stylize" the world beyond our
local environment through manipulation of news. As a result, whole
communities can be brought to see other peoples and groups,
specifically those of which they have no direct local knowledge, in
generally the same artificial way. The result is a thought collective,
which then becomes a vehicle by which communities can be mobi-
lized to act collectively against alleged enemies.

This book will look at one specific negative potential of natural
localness: cultural genocide. As used in this work, cultural genocide
is the purposeful weakening and ultimate destruction of cultural

values and practices of feared out-groups. The goal of cultural genocide can be the withering away of the enemy group, or it might be
the severe impairment of the enemy culture as part of a program to
undermine effective resistance to conquest and domination. One
might think of this approach as follows: if natural localness is a starting point for group identity and cultural solidarity, powerful groups
seeking to attack feared out-groups may well see it as logical to
attempt to destroy the foundations of localness of these enemies.
Thus, short of physical genocide, destruction of the basis for identity
and culture seems to be a viable tactic.

At this point one might ask why a contemporary aggressive and
expansionist group organized into a nation-state and urged on by
prejudices would bother with cultural genocide? Why not just continue the old imperial and colonial practice of physical genocide? An
answer can be suggested, at least in terms of the contemporary West:
the Holocaust still serves as a shock to the system of the Western
powers and prevents them, and perhaps other cultures seeking to
claim affiliation with the West, from practicing or condoning physical genocide.

A Western recognition of the truly existential danger posed by
physical genocide only appeared after World War II, in the after-
math of the Holocaust. Why did it take so long for the West to see
this practice as a manifest danger to itself? It might very well be that
the death camps of World War II, where the technology of modernity that characterized European civilization was turned to the mass
killing of subsets of the Europeans themselves, were too shocking to
rationalize away—particularly given the newsreel pictures of the
concentration camps that were shown often and widely in the West.
In other words, as long as the victims of physical genocide were non-
Europeans, the situation could be rationalized away, or just ignored,
within a distorting thought collective that emphasized economic

necessity and the colonial expansion of the borders of civilization. By the 1930s, however, the Nazis had, in effect, brought the racial stereotyping and prejudice that had made possible colonial slaughter back home to Europe. By inventing the modern Aryan race and designating its primary area of activity to be Europe itself, the Nazis came to see not just the non-Western world but Europe, too, as full of inferior peoples to be bullied, enslaved, or murdered for the benefit of a superior people with its own overweening, locally produced ideological view of things. Under this new order, the Jews were to be genocidally slaughtered, and the Poles and Russians enslaved. And what of western Europeans such as the French? Well, ultimately, they were to be treated by the Nazis in the same manner as the French themselves had treated the native Algerians and Vietnamese. But in 1945, upon the defeat of the master race, the populations of the West were sufficiently shocked over what had taken place in their own backyard that they recognized that there were important lessons to be learned from the Holocaust. This is an issue to which we shall return at the end of this book.

We will now move on to a number of case studies that will show us how cultural genocide against a feared out-group can manifest itself with the popular support of the dominant population. The early cases will be from the years preceding the Holocaust and the later ones will be after that event. In the process we will set the theory laid out above into practice.

2

CULTURAL GENOCIDE AND
THE AMERICAN INDIANS

The theoretical background for our approach to cultural genocide
is the universal phenomenon of natural localness. It is within this
default position that most of us live our daily lives and come to
know and understand our environment. In the case we are about
to consider, the cultural genocide committed against the American
Indians, the local environment of the frontier was one of confrontation between colonists and Indians. The "pictures in our heads" that
evolved in this zone of confrontation did so against the backdrop of
colonial domination of the land and Indian resistance. Away from
this zone, the understanding of the frontier struggle conformed to
the cultural paradigm of the competing parties. Here we will deal
mainly with the outlook of the European colonists, the ones who
perpetrated and supported the assault on American Indian cultures.

The vast majority of colonists had arrived in the Americas with
an assured sense of their own civilizational superiority and quickly
developed a correspondingly negative view of Indian society and
culture. This was so whether the Europeans came to the New World
for religious reasons or economic ones, or whether they came
from England, France, Spain, the Netherlands, Sweden, or elsewhere.
From the colonists' point of view, the Indians' tools and weapons,

their religions, their relative nakedness, their occupations, their family life—all were judged to be of an inferior nature. For the vast number of colonists, this assumption would never be questioned. This primary fact must be borne in mind as we go through the following history.

Thus, both on and off the frontier, the Indians were seen as barbarians and savages who had to give way before colonial expansion, which represented the God-ordained advancement of civilization. The inferior naturally had to give way to the superior. This pervasive assumption, which rapidly became the foundational concept of a colonial thought collective, stood independent of the behavior of this or that set of Indians or colonists. Quite often particular frontier colonists could behave like barbarians (and be recognized as acting so by the government of the Great Britain or the United States), and particular Indian groups could behave in a benign and civilized fashion. It made no difference to the character and power of the evolving thought collective, which readily used emotive language that tapped into hardwired concerns for security against danger and maintenance of community solidarity.

As a result, the colonial media (newspapers), "Indian experts" (often clergymen), and politicians all subscribed to the notion that Indians were enemies and their extinction was justified and inevitable. That meant that the ordinary colonial citizen behind the frontier was immersed in an information environment that reflected and buttressed the thought collective. An important aspect of this situation was that domain or content knowledge about the frontier situation, as well as about Indian life and culture, was superficial and subject to distortion. It was certainly not sufficient to allow the colonists to make an independent critical judgment about the struggle taking place between the two peoples. If one combines the power of the thought collective and the superior strength of the colonists, both in weapons and, in the long run, in numbers, one can see that the position of the Indians was poor in the extreme. Within the colonial society it was not a question of whether the Indians ought to go extinct. The question was how it should occur. Should it be by a process of physical genocide, or by the more "benign" process of cultural genocide?

Early Contacts:
Two Precedent-Setting Examples

The first substantial number of European settlers came to the shores of what is now the United States in the early seventeenth century. Among the best known of the early settlements was the one at Jamestown, established in 1607 by the Virginia Company of London. The initial number of settlers was 105. Within seven months, only thirty-eight survived. This first-season mortality rate was not due to hostile action by indigenous peoples but rather to the malarial environment in which the colony sat, the lack of adequate drinking water, and an underestimation of the sheer hard work it would take to endure in a wilderness. Indeed, the European population in Virginia would not be able to sustain its own numbers until the end of the seventeenth century. Until that time it had to rely on a steady stream of new immigrants (mostly in the form of indentured servants) just to stave off extinction.

Relations with the local Indians, the Powhatan (who numbered about fourteen thousand at the time of Jamestown was founded), was at first mutually beneficial. The initial settlers needed food to survive, and the Indians desired metal tools. However, relations eventually deteriorated because, as their numbers stabilized and began to grow through immigration, the colonists spread out. As they did so, they asserted their alien view of private property in land,

and intruded on ever more Indian territory. Given their a priori
assumption of superiority, they also often behaved in a way that
threatened and offended their Indian neighbors (Puglisi 1991). The
chief of the Powhatan soon expressed the conviction that the English
had come "not for trade, but to invade my people and possess my
country" (Vaughn 1978). Hostilities led to the First Anglo-Powhatan
War. Retaliation and resistance by the Indians led to a series of massacres of English settlers in 1622 that killed about one-third of the
colony's population. The Powhatan seemed to have assumed that
such a powerful blow would convince the English to abandon the
settlement altogether. The settlers did not go away, however, but
increased greatly in number. Subsequent warfare, which involved an
effort by the English to starve the Indians through the destruction of
their cornfields, forced the Powhatan to negotiate a peace. At the
peace ceremony, the Jamestown leadership proceeded to poison
the drink given to the Indian representatives, killing 157 of them
(Roundtree 1996, 77). It was a sign that, at least among the Jamestown
elite, hatred for the Indians ran deep enough that they did not
consider peaceful cohabitation as a real option. Physical genocide
seemed to have been considered a potential ultimate solution. There
is little doubt that the Powhatan would have pursued a similar end
if they could.

The "problem" for both sides was that physical genocide was not
easily achievable. When in 1644 renewed warfare broke out, the
Powhatan killed some five hundred colonists. But this now represented less than 10 percent of the English population. The Indians
were not only out-gunned but they were out-manned by a continuous inflow of European immigrants. The colonists (depending
on the region of settlement) were often diverted from wholesale
genocide by religious scruples and/or labor needs. Enslavement
(later removal) and Christian conversion were strong competing

solutions to extermination. As early as 1610, the Virginia Company executives in London had directed the governor of the colony, Sir Thomas Gates, to Christianize the natives (Roundtree 1996, 54).

From the mid-1640s onward, the Powhatan and other Indian groups in the Virginia region suffered continuous decline. Their fate was to be herded into smaller and smaller territory or forced farther west. Those who remained within communication range of the English settlers would be subject to a process of relentless cultural genocide through religious conversion and concentration in "praying Indian towns" or colonial Indian schools. From the colonial point of view, such a "civilizing" process would by definition reduce resistance to ongoing settlement.

Further north, in what would become New England, there were also eventual clashes with the indigenous peoples and for many of the same reasons as found in Virginia. The Pilgrims came over on the *Mayflower* in December 1620 and founded the Plymouth settlement. They too numbered about one hundred, and again half would die within the first year of settlement. Diseases such as scurvy were a major cause of this initial mortality. Those who survived were soon reinforced from England. The New England settlers, like those farther south, followed the pattern of spreading out from their central colony, thus encroaching on more and more of the land the local Indians used for hunting, gathering, and fishing. What would become New Hampshire was established in 1623. Connecticut was being settled by 1633, and Rhode Island got its start in 1636. In addition, during this time, the Dutch established New Amsterdam (which would later be New York) and then proceeded to expand up the Hudson Valley. The Swedes came to what is now Delaware, and the Calvert family, who were English Catholics, began to create Maryland. Plymouth was destined to be absorbed into the Massachusetts Bay Colony. By 1642, there were some twelve thousand Europeans in the general area of Plymouth. The inflow of setters was like a great uncontrollable tidal wave.

The *Mayflower* colonists had some early tense encounters with the local Indians during their first winter and so, by February 1621, they had created a militia under the command of Myles Standish. For their part, the Wampanoag and Patuxet Indians of the region had prior contact with English fishermen operating offshore and had suffered occasional violent attacks as well as outbreaks of European diseases such as smallpox. Thus they were wary of the *Mayflower* settlers. Nonetheless, in March 1621, the Wampanoag chief, Massasoit, and those of other tribes as well, made an agreement with the colonists to the effect that neither would act in ways that would harm the other. Obviously, the settlers did not see their own expansion (that is the expansion of civilization) as a harmful act.

As early as the summer of 1622, the expansion of European settlement created the circumstances for a breakdown of peaceful relations between the Pilgrims and their Indian neighbors. The colonial outpost of Wessagussett reported to Plymouth that they were under threat from local Indians, and Myles Standish led a militia contingent to defend the outpost. Standish soon learned that no attack had occurred. Instead of seeking a peaceful resolution of whatever tensions there were, Standish decided that the local Indians needed to learn greater fear of the settlers and so launched what today we would call a preemptive strike. According to the account of "Standish's raid" given by historian Nathaniel Philbrick, the famous Plymouth leader invited two of the local Indian leaders to Wessagussett for a meal and, getting them inside one of the cabins, proceeded to stab them to death (it probably never occurred to him simply to poison them). Philbrick concludes, in something of an understatement, that "Standish's raid had irreparably damaged the human ecology of the region" (Philbrick 2006, 151–155). Many of the local Indians did leave the area out of fear of Standish's actions, but belatedly the colonists realized that they had only hurt themselves by their rash actions. At this time the main source of the Plymouth colony's income was the trade in furs. With the withdrawal of many of the local Indians, the fur trade quickly dried up.

Intermittent fighting occurred over the next fifty years. At this time, the English were assisted by outbreaks of disease among their Indian enemies. These were seen as acts of God. Looking back on one episode during this time, the preacher Increase Mather tells us that around 1631 problems with the local "quarrelsome" natives was ended by "God . . . sending the Smallpox amongst the Indians of Saugust" (Thorton 1990, 75). The culmination of this Puritan-Indian conflict was King Philip's War, which began in 1675. The general cause of the war was, again, the expansion of English settlers into Indian territory. There was also the use of force to coerce the local Wampanoag Indians to sell some of their land to the new English town of Swansea (Kawashima 1986, 205–224). Around 8 percent of the English adult population died during the ensuing struggle, but this was nothing compared to Indian losses. It is estimated that the Indian population of the entire New England region fell by some 60 to 80 percent (Philbrick 2006, 332, 345–346).

The experiences of the American Indians who came into contact with both the Jamestown and Plymouth colonies was the norm for other Indian groups, not only in this relatively early period but in later years as well. Colonial expansion assured that contact led to tension and eventual hostilities. The result was Indian defeat and ethnic cleansing. As a result, in the areas adjacent to the Chesapeake River and Massachusetts Bay, the number of native American villages was minute by 1700. Yet, as we will see, the violence entailed in the purging of the Indians created the lasting image of who they were in the minds of the dominant colonial population.

NATURAL LOCALNESS AND THE EVOLVING
IMAGE OF THE INDIAN

By 1700, the American frontier was already receding westward. And, as the century wore on, the probability of any European resident of the eastern coastal region encountering an Indian lessened steadily. John Adams, the second president of the United States, wrote to Thomas Jefferson, who would be his successor, on June 28, 1812, that, seventy years previously (around 1742), his father had frequent encounters with two eminent Indian acquaintances of the still surviving Neponset tribe. They would visit Adams's house in what is now Quincy, Massachusetts (part of the greater Boston area). But now, in 1812, Adams remarks that "not a soul is left. We scarcely see an Indian in a year" (Cappon 1959, 310–311). Ralph Waldo Emerson, writing in his journal in 1845, stated that "We in Massachusetts see the Indians only as a picturesque antiquity" (Dippie 1982, 32). The fact is that the Indians were always a frontier phenomenon. The farther one lived from the frontier the more the American Indians slipped into obscurity because they were no longer part of the common person's local reality. Thus, they were not thought about on a daily basis and when they did enter consciousness it was through the vehicle of "stylized news."

How was the Indian portrayed to the "white man" living east of the frontier? The sources of information for the average colonist/ American would have been newspapers, literature, and the public pronouncements of those white men offering themselves as "experts." The images that were offered had the overarching theme of fated Indian demise. That is, the Indian was vanishing by virtue of an ordained destiny. As one U.S. senator poetically put it in 1825, "Like a promontory of sand, exposed to the ceaseless encroachments of the ocean, they have been gradually wasting away before the current of the white population." It represented "inexorable destiny" or "the extinction of our savage precursors before the dawn of science and cultivation" (Dippie 1982, 13).

Popular opinion of how destined extinction would come upon the American Indian varied with circumstances, however. Thus, according to Brian W. Dippie in his excellent book *The Vanishing American: White Attitudes and U.S. Indian Policy*, the eighteenth-century outlook on this subject was initially influenced by Enlightenment thought, which favored the belief that the fate of the Indian was to be assimilated into European culture. This act of benign cultural genocide would be achieved by initially converting the Indians, all of whom were allegedly barbarian hunter-gatherers, into farmers and/or town dwellers. That many of the Indians encountered by the settlers of Plymouth and Jamestown had in fact been at least part—time farmers and lived in villages that resembled small towns was already forgotten. Dippie attributes this assimilationist assumption to the prevailing influence of John Locke's theory of tabula rasa (Dippie 1982, 4). That is, we are all born blank slates and essentially equal. At birth there is no inherent difference between an Indian infant and the baby destined to be the king of England. What will make them different is their subsequent experience. Change the experiences of the American Indian and you change the Indian into something else. Thomas Jefferson, whose outlook was certainly shaped by Enlightenment thought, expressed the opinion that the Indians could be "improved" and would eventually be brought into "civilization" (Dippie 1982, 5).

Meanwhile, on the frontier, the Indian was offering stubborn and often violent resistance to colonial encroachment. This was so even though Jefferson, and no doubt most white observers away from the frontier, perceived Indian loss of land as due to the tribes' "voluntary sales" of their territory (Dippie 1982, 33). Nonetheless, it was the defeat of the Indian tribes at the Battle of Fallen Timbers in 1794 that led to the loss of their lands to the north and west of the Ohio River. The pressure put on the Cherokees, Chickasaws, and Creeks meant their loss of lands in the region of Tennessee and Georgia. Jefferson interpreted this, too, as destiny. "While they [the Indians] are learning to do better [as farmers] on less land, our increasing numbers will be calling for more land, and thus a coincidence of interests will be produced between those who have lands to spare, and want other necessities, and those who have such necessaries to spare, and want lands" (Dippie 1982, 5).

Jefferson, of course, was not residing on the frontier, and one can assume that colonial attitudes altered as one approached the zone of resistance. But a process of popularizing the attitudes of this frontier zone among those behind the lines, so to speak, now took place. For instance, in the early years of the French and Indian War (1754–1755), colonial newspapers kept up a steady flow of reports about Indian attacks along the frontier. These were replete with descriptions of torture and brutality. According to these reports, the Indians in such areas as western Pennsylvania had been seduced away from friendship with the benign British colonists by the nefarious French (Copeland 1997, 6). The predictable result was that "newspaper accounts of the war created a fear of both the French and Indians that was not entirely justified." The English forces, on the other hand were described to the colonial reader as the eighteenth-century version of "freedom fighters" (Copeland 1997, 11). Such use of the newspapers to spread war propaganda essentially brought the frontier picture of the Indian as an incorrigible and barbaric enemy eastward into regions where the American Indian was otherwise absent from daily colonial life. It also eroded the assimilationist position that the Indians could be "changed for the better." This negative portrayal of the Indian was repeated at the time of the American Revolution and the War of 1812.

During the French and Indian War, it was logical for most of the Indians to favor the French side. The French had not settled in the New World in as great numbers as the English colonists had, and so the French had not created the constant and deleterious frontier pressure the English were exerting. Moreover, during the Revolution and the War of 1812, most of the surviving Indians east of the Mississippi River fought with the British against the Americans. This too was logical, because the British government was no longer associated with that frontier, as the American settlers emphatically still were.

Although the Indian choice of allies was logical, from the American perspective it made them an enemy many times over. The portrayal of the frontier Indians as "bloody savages," instead of "noble savages," was now repeated from the local newspapers, pulpits, and political platforms all the way up to President James Madison, who declared that despite a "just and benevolent" policy toward the Indians, the red man had repaid the frontier settler with a "savage thirst for blood" and the practice of "torture and death on maimed and defenseless captives" (Dippie 1982, 6). It should be emphasized that most of the local stylizers of news, and the president as well, did not see themselves as distorting the facts. Their perceptions were shaped by a cultural paradigm that, as noted, represented whites as agents of civilization and even agents of God. The colonists were good people. The Indians were agents of barbarism. They were hopelessly bad people. Thus when, during the peace negotiations that ended the War of 1812, a British representative told the American negotiators that their government's record of relations toward the frontier Indians completely ignored the Indians' right to land, "thereby menacing a final extinction of those nations," the Americans were reported to have reacted as if they were insulted. No, they declared, American policy had always been "humane and liberal" (Nash 1974, 62 and 126). It had always been a civilizing policy.

As a consequence of perceived Indian behavior, by the end of the War of 1812 increasing numbers of Americans did not see Jefferson's path to assimilation as an acceptable answer to the "Indian problem." And, indeed, Jefferson's position had always been based on a false assumption that the Indians would voluntarily trade their alleged surplus of land for the white man's surplus of trinkets and tools. Having found out that this was not the case, his countrymen simply went to the other extreme, coming to the conclusion that the Indians were congenitally savage, "depraved from birth" (Dippie 1982, 7). This pervasive public opinion would persist through the nineteenth century and support the notion that the Indians were doomed to vanish. Of the myriad novels about the American Indian published in the nineteenth century, including those of James Fenimore Cooper, all taught that the Indians were fated to physical extinction (Dippie 1982, 21). This act of popular wishful thinking would challenge those few who sought to promote "humane and liberal" approaches, such as the conversion of the Indians to good Christian yeoman farmers, and thus save them from physical genocide through the vehicle of cultural genocide. The Indians would resist both.

How Would the Vanishing American Vanish?

Thus it was that white men and women throughout the colonies, and then United States, developed a thought-collective picture of the Indians. That is, by 1815, generally similar pictures of the Indians could be found among the local, regional, and national population. Keep in mind that, as time went by, most Americans had no first-hand knowledge of Indians. And the stylization of news about the

Indian across the media spectrum, which the majority ingested for over a century, was consistent and mostly negative. The news of a vanishing race of barbarians was sufficient to have "anesthetized the listener's conscience" and made the notion of the inevitable extinction of the Indian a "habit of thought" (Dippie 1982, 15). Once this shared perspective was in place, there was a natural tendency to reinforce it by seeking out information that supported it. Contradictory facts were ignored or downplayed. Thus in the 1820s and 1830s the case of the Cherokee Indians and their successful adaptation to farming and other aspects of white "civilization" (they were anxious "to learn English so that the white man cannot cheat us"; McLoughlin 1984, 52–53) was dismissed and denied. The white man coveted Cherokee land. And adhering to the image of Indian savagery that was central to the paradigm of the thought collective facilitated its theft. It was a more or less perfect paradigmatic cover-up.

Thought collectives often transform stereotypes and unanalyzed assertions into firmly implanted assumptions of truth. This applies to white American perceptions of the Indian in the seventeenth through nineteenth centuries. That in this process there was a war of extermination going on was, as a consequence, easily rationalized away.

One of the primary rationalizations was that the flawed character of the American Indians was the source of their own demise. They were essentially committing racial suicide by drinking themselves to death, by contracting Old World diseases (which was a mark of their inferiority), and by their warlike culture. But most of all they were killing themselves by virtue of their inability to become "civilized."

The Indians were fated to be vanquished by the stronger civilization of the white man. They were doomed to fall before "progress," just like their forest and plains habitats. Moreover, every time the Indian came into contact with that civilization it proved fatal to him. As James Fenimore Cooper put it, "by mixing with us . . . [the Indians] imbibe only our vices, without emulating our virtues—and our intercourse with them is decisively disadvantageous to them" (Dippie 1982, 25). Government officials agreed with this analysis. President James Monroe put it this way, "Experience has clearly demonstrated that independent savage communities can not long exist within the limits of a civilized population. . . . Pressed on every side by the white population" they would become drunkards or fall to the white man's diseases (Dippie 1982, 48). Therefore, for the Indians' own good, to preserve them from inevitable extinction as long as possible, they had to be segregated from white society. And, the only way to do that was to dispossess them of what was left of their ancestral lands and remove them to someplace beyond the ever-expanding frontier. As Henry Schoolcraft, an "Indian expert" put it in 1838, "it is now evident to all that the salvation of these interesting relics of Oriental races lie in colonization west. . . . Public sentiment has settled on that ground; sound policy dictates it; and the most enlarged philanthropy for the Indian race perceives its best hopes in the measure" (Dippie 1982, 48). This was the part of the thought collective paradigm that exonerated the civilized white man for his behavior toward the Indians and put all the blame on his victim.

It is interesting to note that many of those, both within and without the American government, who knew that the expansion of their society was exterminating the Indian, sought to use the time these doomed people had left for the project of memorializing them through art. This seemed to be the mission of the self-taught painter George Catlin (1796–1872). Catlin sought to record in portraiture the "uncorrupted" Indian who as yet lived beyond the reach of white settlement. He did this with the full knowledge that these Indians could not avoid the "grand and irresistible march of civilization" and remain "uncorrupted" (Catlin 1973, 1: 156). And so he described his mission as "a monument to a dying race" (Roehm 1966, 442). In his career Catlin visited forty-eight different tribes and produced about 470 paintings. However, this was not only the mission of a man with empathy for the American Indian. It was also part of a perverse exercise on the part of the U.S. government—specifically the War Department. Starting in the 1820s, the same government department that had the mission of dispossessing and segregating the Indian took up the task of collecting a large number of paintings of their victims so as to be able to answer the future question, as Secretary of War James Barbour put it, "What sort of being was the red man of America?" (Dippie 1982, 27).

All of this was possible because the prevailing thought collective of white Americans associated their expansion across the continent with "progress." This expansion was irresistible and inevitable. Indeed, it was so because it was ordained by God. As U.S. Representative Richard H. Wilde put it during the Twenty-first Session of Congress in 1829, "Jacob will forever obtain the inheritance of Esau. We cannot alter the laws of Providence, as we read them in the experience of the ages" (Weinberg 1963, 85). The Bible made it clear that the earth belonged to those who could make it "fruitful," and it was America's "manifest destiny" to make it so. As the influential Harvard Professor Edward Everett explained in 1823, "The Europeans came; and—by causes as simple and natural as they are innocent— the barbarous population . . . has been replaced by one much better, much happier." Their demise was therefore the product of "the unavoidable operation of natural causes" (Dippie 1982, 30). It is amazing how civilized man can forgo free will when it is to his advantage.

Under these conditions, removal and segregation of the Indians became the official policy of the U.S. government after 1812. This was, perhaps, thought of as an alternative to physical extermination.

But, from the position described above, this assumption would be only a psychological ploy. For if the expansion of civilization was inevitable and the Indian incapable of adaptation, then an eventual vanishing of the race was the logical end product. Yet there were always a minority that believed there were alternatives. The Indian could be saved from physical extinction by transforming at least some of them, individually, into civilized folk. Reeducation of the young and Christianizing those who were willing could save a select few Indians. Cultural genocide, therefore, was both possible and a preferable alternative to physical genocide.

CHRISTIANIZING AND EDUCATING THE INDIANS

As noted, most Americans lived away from the frontier and did not witness the behavior of their compatriots that led to the fierce resistance of the Indian. There were, of course, a select number who suspected, as one government report put it in 1876, that "when the true history of the Indian wrongs is laid before our countrymen, their united voice will demand that the honor and interests of the nation shall no longer be sacrificed to the insatiable lust and avarice of unscrupulous [white] men" (Tinker 1993, 106). However, by that time it would be safe to condemn the avarice, for the policies of expropriation would have been completed, "leaving no further temptation" (Weinberg 1963, 73). In the meantime, most Americans accepted as true the stylized news that attributed the fierceness to the Indians to their congenital barbarian character. This conclusion was a function of a lack of accurate contextual knowledge about the Indian's situation on the part the white majority. The fact that the colonial majority did not know what the frontier minority were doing to the Indians (an ignorance that continues to plague Americans when it comes to their modern foreign policy) allowed most Americans, from the president on down to the average citizen, to truly believe that the government's Indian policy was "humane and liberal." Dispossessing the Indians and segregating them westward for their own good was part of this policy. Encouraging missionary work and education among the safely removed savages (as futile as this might prove) was another.

Earlier, in the seventeenth century, Puritan missionaries had established fourteen "praying towns" for Indian coverts. In these towns some eleven hundred Indians were instructed in the Christian faith, the "habits of industry [farming]," and the English language. Most of these towns were destroyed during King Philip's War (1675–1676) and other clashes between Europeans and the local Indians. During this period, Bibles were also translated into a number of Indian dialects, and there was limited success in training a few Indians to be Christian preachers (Reyhner and Eder 2004, 26–27). The effort continued into the eighteenth and nineteenth centuries (spurred on by the Second Great Awakening), with the emphasis now on Indian children. For instance, the missionary Eleazar Wheelock promoted removal of Indian children of both sexes to Moor's Indian Charity School in Lebanon, Connecticut. Wheelock was interested in saving the Indians' souls, but was also shrewd enough to argue that "missionaries and schoolmasters were cheaper than fortresses and wars" (Reyhner and Eder 2004, 31). The record of achievement of this effort was not good, however. Toward the end of his life he wrote, "I have turned out forty Indians who were good readers, writers, and instructed in the Christian religion. . . . By contact with the vices of their tribes, not more than half preserved their characters unstained" (Layman 1942, 92).

Toward the end of the eighteenth century, and after America gained its independence, Congress declared that "the utmost good faith shall always be observed towards the Indians, their lands and property shall never be taken from them without their consent; and in their property, rights and liberty they shall never be invaded or disturbed, unless in just and lawful wars authorized by Congress" (Reyhner and Eder 2004, 40). And, indeed, President George Washington, in his fourth annual address to Congress in 1792, urged the legislators to provide sufficient funds to enforce laws along the frontier and thereby "restrain the commission of outrages upon the Indians" (Reyhner and Eder 2004, 41). This message went against the prevailing thought collective, however, and so, history tells us, this effort was never adequately undertaken.

Such inaction frustrated, but did not stop, the minority of nineteenth-century whites who still believed that, as the missionary Jedidiah Morse put it in 1820, "effectual measures be taken to bring them [the Indians] over this awful gulf, to the solid and safe ground of civilization" (Morse 1822, 66). Of course this meant that the Indians would have to become "praying Indians" and yeoman farmers, or something wholly other than what they originally were. In this effort, the "principles of the Christian religion" would continue to be combined with the promotion of "useful arts" such as farming and husbandry. To this end, Protestant missionaries began to establish "model Zions" in the frontier areas early in the nineteenth century. These were "manual-labor boarding schools" in which Indian children could be housed, converted, and made into farmers while free from the "influence of their heathen parents" (Reyhner and Eder 2004, 50).

One other notion that was to be instilled into these children was the desire for private property. Lewis Henry Morgan, America's foremost anthropologist and leading "expert" on the Indians in the mid-nineteenth century, told his fellows that "it is impossible to overestimate the influence of property in the civilization of mankind," and that the drive to own property had "unimaginable power" to

jump-start the process of civilizing the Indian, because "its dominance as a passion over all other passions marks the commencement
of civilization" (Morgan 1877, 3–8). According to Brian Dippie, the
move toward private property, particularly in land, was also seen as
a way to "break up existing tribal units" (Dippie 1982, 111). And
these, of course, were the units upon which resistance to white
encroachment was based.

The missionaries lobbied the U.S. government, and in 1818 a
House Committee noted that "in the present state of our country,
one of two things seems necessary: either that these sons of the
forest should be moralized or exterminated" (Prucha 1984, 150).
The government, under pressure from the missionaries, opted to
attempt the former, and in 1819 President Monroe signed into law
the Indian Civilization Act, which provided an annual stipend of
$10,000 to subsidize organizations involved in civilizing the Indians.
The missionaries were among those who used this money to staff
the existing fourteen Indian schools with 508 students. Within five
years, the number of schools had grown to twenty-one, with 800
students. Funding for this effort would continue through 1873.

As it turned out, one of the things the government hoped the
teachers and missionaries they were funding would do is convince
the Indians to remove themselves to reservations (Reyhner and Eder
2004, 43–44). That they usually did not do this, but rather opposed
removal, caused repeated protests by those who wished to steal
Indian land officially. For instance, the state of Georgia forced missionaries out of the Cherokee nation territory in 1838 and arrested
those who refused to leave. One, the Reverend Mr. Worcester,
was sentenced to four years at hard labor by a Georgia court for
supporting the Cherokee cause (Reyhner and Eder 2004, 49).

In 1824 the Office of Indian Affairs was set up within the War
Department (and transferred to the Department of Interior in 1849).

The office created annual reports that monitored the effort at Indian education. By 1836, the office report listed fifty-two schools with 1,381 students, concentrated on teaching "farming and homemaking." Missionaries continued to be the major source of staffing for these establishments (Reyhner and Eder 2004, 46). The effort at Christianizing and bringing white education to the Indian went on with more or less enthusiasm through the rest of the nineteenth century. The disillusionment and mistrust that came from the consistently applied policy of Indian removal undercut the missionary efforts, however. It was a strange situation that resulted, though one readily admitted by various U.S. government investigatory commissions. For instance, after the Civil War a Peace Commission, which included Commissioner for Indian Affairs Nathaniel Taylor and General William T. Sherman, among others, brought in an 1867 report that spelled out a seminal problem: "While it cannot be denied that the government of the United States, in general terms and temper of its legislation, has evinced a desire to deal generously with the Indians, it must be admitted that the actual treatment they have received has been unjust and iniquitous beyond the power of words to express. Taught by the government that they had rights entitled to respect; when those rights have been assailed by the rapacity of the white man, the arm which should have been raised to protect them has been every ready to sustain the aggressor. The history of the Government connections with the Indians is a shameful record of broken treaties and unfulfilled promises" (Dippie 1982, 60). Whatever one might think of the statement's initial claim, it did lay out the inherent hypocrisy of official behavior toward the Indians over literally hundreds of years.

Ironically, from their own religious perspective, the missionaries did accomplish something even within this horrid environment. As time went on, growing numbers of Indians did identify themselves as Christians. Of course, this utterly failed to enhance their economic or political freedom or ultimate assimilation into white society. Given all the hopes and dreams of generations of missionaries, why was this so? Perhaps it was because "the great mass of the [white] community" never did believe that the missionary effort would work among this "inferior race of men." As one missionary put it at the time, "There seems to be a deep rooted superstition . . . that the Indians are really destined, as if there were some fatality in the case, never to be Christianized, but gradually to decay till they become totally extinct" (Dippie 1982, 10). The superstition was wholly self-serving. President Washington's secretary of war, Henry Knox, stated bluntly that the attitude that found civilizing the Indians to be "impracticable" was "probably more convenient than just" (Mohr 1933, 172). And we have seen that when it came to the land of the Cherokees in Georgia, the Indian ability to live in a "civilized" fashion was irrelevant. The truth is that the majority of white society, living apart from the historical processes impacting the Indians, never lost the paradigmatic picture of the Indian as a barbarian. Nor did their media and politicians disabuse them; countervailing official reports were not publicly disseminated. And it may very well be that the majority would have been indifferent to the fact that the savage was turning Christian even if they were made aware of it. For those who did pay attention, apart from a few missionaries and humanitarians, the Indian was and had to remain a savage, because it was much harder to dispossess an assimilated citizen.

Conclusion

As the historian George E. Tinker tells us, there was always a strong undercurrent of opinion that favored the physical extermination of the Indians among colonial and later America frontier settlers, as well as elements of the U.S. military (Tinker 1993, 98). The characterization of the Indians as bloody savages that came from the press and politicians of the day, operating within an environment of natural localness and a lack of accurate contextual knowledge, had early on created a thought collective among the general population that probably would have supported such a process of physical genocide. That this did not occur in any quick and overt fashion was because: 1) there was always plenty of land beyond the frontier into which to remove and concentrate the natives; this gave rise to the reservation policy; and 2) there was also a religious and humanitarian minority who, from the beginning of settlement, argued that the "Indian problem" could be remedied through a cultural and religious conversion process rather than physical genocide.

In most cases, these individuals were sincere in their efforts to force the Indians to become white men. For instance, Tinker, in his book *Missionary Conquest*, tells the story of Henry Benjamin Whipple, who was elected Episcopal bishop of Minnesota in 1859. Whipple was "a man of the highest moral character who had only the best intentions." However, his single-minded effort to force the Sioux Indians into American society by teaching them to be yeoman farmers, advocates of private property, and good Christians only left them "oppressed and dysfunctional." Nonetheless, Whipple was convinced that without assimilation the Sioux and other American Indians were doomed to extinction (Tinker 1993, 95, 103). The fact was, as Tinker makes clear, that this more "humane and just" process amounted to one of cultural genocide (Tinker 1993, 99). At the time, of course, it was not thought of in that way. So, where is sin to be found? In the intention that brings forth the act or only in the consequences of the act?

The ultimate goal of the white settler population and the government that represented it was always to acquire the land upon which the various American Indian tribes lived. This was an end the "civi-lizing" missionaries could not successfully oppose and, more often than not, they accepted it as inevitable. Most of them agreed that the confiscation of Indian land was to be equated with the march of civilization. And, as long as the missionary efforts at assimilation did not get in the way of the policy of Indian removal, the U.S. government allowed it to go forward. Where the missionaries did get in the way, as in the case of the Cherokees, they were simply removed from the scene.

In all of this there was little comment and less protest from the majority of Americans. Encased in their localness, they did not think very much about the fate of the Indians. Indeed, whether they went physically extinct or culturally extinct was a function of how they, the Indians, chose to react to the "inevitability" of advancing civilization—an inevitability that was ordained by God. This pat scenario, where the victims decide on the nature of their own demise, is repeated again and again in history. And the choice is often the same: physical extermination or cultural genocide.

3

RUSSIA AND THE
JEWS IN THE
NINETEENTH CENTURY

The theoretical considerations put forth in chapter 1 are universal in applicability and should be borne in mind in our consideration of particular episodes involving cultural genocide. The interplay of natural localness (which inherently limits our ability to bring accurate contextual knowledge to the understanding of nonlocal events) and the popular stylizing of news allow for the manipulation of attitudes and behaviors about nonlocal subjects. Such manipulation can impact the beliefs and behavior of a large percentage of any given population. The vehicles for this manipulation are the government and managed media of the age in question and the use of emotive language as well as the presentation of "expert opinion." The end product of this manipulation is the thought collective.

This process operated in the history of the European settlement of the Americas and in the westward expansion of the United States. It created the thought collective necessary for the dispossession, segregation, and near extermination of the Native American population. It also created the attitudes that argued against physical genocide and for the imposition of cultural genocide.

We now turn to a very different historical milieu for our second example. It is set not in the New World, but the Old World. It takes up a situation characterized not so much by a clash of life styles as one of religions—those of Christians and Jews in nineteenth-century Russian-controlled territory. However, as in the case of the American Indians, here too segregation plays a role and, in the interplay of the competing groups, one finds wavering between physical genocide and cultural genocide.

Russia's Anti-Semitic Thought Collective, Part One

Jews have been part of the Russian demographic landscape for a very long time. Documented evidence of small Jewish communities in areas that once constituted the southern region of the Soviet Union go back to the fourth century C.E. (Dubnow 1918, 1:1–3). Whether one believes or disbelieves that Khazars, who once ruled southern Russia, Kazakhstan, and parts of the Ukraine, constituted a Jewish kingdom in the early ninth century, there can be little doubt that by that time the Jewish population in the region had grown substantially. They probably spread north and west in the tenth and eleventh centuries. Meanwhile, other Jews then resident in western and central Europe moved eastward in the twelfth century as a consequence of late medieval anti-Jewish persecution, increasing the general Jewish population in territories that evolved into the Grand Duchy of Moscow. In the fourteenth century, Jews were being expelled from Western European kingdoms such as England, France, and Spain, and some of them went to what was then the evolving Polish kingdom of Casimir III. Later this territory would later come under the rule of an expanding Russian empire.

As the Jewish population of what would become Russia grew, the bulk of the Jews did not assimilate with the gentile community. They were seen, both by themselves and others, as a stand-alone

religious community with its own traditions and culture. This culture evolved within the environment of the shtetl or Jewish town.
Within the shtetls, the language was some variant on Yiddish, the
laws were drawn from religious sources (*halakha*), and there existed
a distinctly "us and them" attitude toward the surrounding gentile
population. This segregation of the communities had a major effect
on the role of natural localness in the evolving perceptions each
group held of the other. Particularly in the case of the gentile
community, it allowed for perceptions of the Jews to be dominated
by negative myth and stereotype.

The origins of these myths and stereotypes no doubt had much
to do with the gentile understanding (or misunderstanding) of the
roots of Christianity. We now know that Jesus was a Jewish preacher
within the apocalyptic subculture prevalent in the Palestine of
his day. He went to Jerusalem during the Passover feast to preach
repentance in the face of what he believed was the imminent end of
the world. There he was identified as a troublemaker by the Jewish
community leaders. They had experienced similar preachers in the
past whose apocalyptic sermons had led to riots. Fearing popular
disturbances, these community leaders shared their fears with the
Roman authorities. It is the latter who arrested Jesus and quickly
executed him (Ehrman 1999). Unfortunately, this history evolved
into a myth that identified the Jews as "Christ killers." This myth
ingrained itself strongly within the popular lore of the Christian
communities of Europe and helped produce, in that localized
and segregated environment, the "pictures in the heads" of many
gentiles. As we will see, this was certainly the case in Russia, where
Eastern Orthodox Christianity became a pillar of Russian identity
and anti-Semitism often became a policy of the state.

This myth of the Jews as Christ killers and the consequent
popular anti-Semitism not only contributed to the segregation of

the Jews from the gentile communities but also to restricted access to nonagricultural occupations. Typical of this situation was that when Casimir III invited the Jews into fourteenth-century Poland, he did so with the intention of having them become a commercial and middleman class performing such specialized duties as tax and toll collection and money lending (Christians were discouraged from engaging in banking at this time). These specialty professions for the Jews were typical of the European economic arrangements for this era. They, in turn, intensified a culturally embedded belief that the Jews were not only enemies of the Christian religion (being the killers of Christ), but also economic exploiters of the majority non-noble population (being money lenders as well as tax and toll collectors). The emotive language used to promote these concepts by both church and state were consistently negative and given to increasingly exaggerated claims about Jewish behavior, of which the infamous "blood libel" (allegations that Jews killed gentile children to use their blood in rituals) is but one example. It made the Jews, as a group, subject to the charge that they were a "parasitic element" preying on the peasantry. And it made them vulnerable to periodic attack by the population at large—attacks that were sometimes encouraged by government officials looking for scapegoats.

Thus anti-Semitism was not a class-based affair but pervaded all elements of society, top to bottom. Keep in mind Daniel T. Willingham's statement (in chapter 1) that "the processes of thinking are intertwined with the content of thought." We can only understand the world and act in it on the basis of what we know. What the bulk of the Russian people, as well as their leaders, knew of the Jews was a product of distorted information. This is the Russian variant of Walter Lippman's "pictures in our heads." That misleading information was, nonetheless, believed real, and policy and behavior was based upon it. The Russian media, often state directed, stylized the news regarding Jews by using harsh and negatively emotive language (as described by Keith Oatley above). What evolved out of this history, and nowhere so strongly as in Russia, is an anti-Semitic thought collective. Like social scientist Arjun Appadurai, we can characterize that thought collective as one of the "severe pathologies" embedded in the "sacred ideologies of nationhood."

Russia's Anti-Semitic Thought Collective, Part Two

We will pick up the story of this thought collective in the reign of Catherine II, the Great (reigned 1762–1796). A standard biography of Catherine depicts her as a liberal for her time (Madariaqa 2002). That is, she is described as ruler who wished to continue the process of Russia's modernization along the model of Western Europe (she was, in fact, of German birth).There was one Russian tradition that she was never able to overcome, however—a nationwide prejudice against the Jews. According to the historian Herman Rosenthal, Catherine was an exception to the general rule of anti-Semitism within the Russian environment (Rosenthal 2002; there will be one more exception among the czars later on). Soon after her coronation, the empress wanted to allow non-Russians, including Jews, greater access to Russian territories for the purpose of building up trade. A restricted version of this edict, which excluded the Jews, was issued in December of 1762. The exclusion is believed to have been forced upon the new empress, who personally saw no reason to keep the Jews out of the traditional Russian lands. Where possible, she did make local exceptions for Jewish individuals, carefully avoiding their identification with a nationally scorned group. In 1769, Catherine sought to allow groups of Jews to settle "the deserted south Russian steppes." In the end, however, the empress had to restrict Jewish residence to the famous "Pale of Settlement," an area of western Russia stretching roughly from Lithuania south through Poland, into the Ukraine, and down to the shores of the Black Sea. The important thing to note is that the opposition to Catherine's liberal attitude to the Jews was ubiquitous. It was not limited to the Orthodox Christian interests, which had supported her accession to the throne. It also came from local town councils, provincial governors, and the Russian Senate at St. Petersburg.

It was also under Catherine's reign that privately owned printing presses were legally imported into Russia. With this, however, came official state censorship that made illegal any publication against "the laws of God and the state" (*Russian History Encyclopedia* 2004). State censorship was continuous from this time until shortly before the Russian Revolution of 1917. As we will see, anti-Semitic writings were not censored out of the Russian press and magazines, and would contribute to the information environment that led to periodic pogroms.

Catherine died in 1796, and after the brief reign of her son Paul, Russia came under the rule of Alexander I (reigned 1801–1825). In 1802 Alexander, who otherwise had his hands full with an aggressive Napoleon Bonaparte, created an advisory council to consider the "Jewish question" in Russia. Out of their deliberations came the Jewish Statute of 1804. At first glance the provisions of this statue seem to be progressive ones that favor the Jews. For instance, within the Pale, it allowed Jewish children access to Russian public schools, freedom to purchase land in "unpopulated areas," the right to "establish factories of all kinds," and commanded that the Jews were not to be "coerced or disturbed . . . in matters of their religious practices and in civilian life generally" ("Statutes Concerning the Organization of the Jews" 1804). However, if one looks into the motivation of the statutes and what they also prohibit, the picture becomes less positive.

As to motivation, the opening preamble explains that the czar was responding to the country's popular thought collective when it came to the Jews. "Numerous complaints have been submitted to us regarding the abuse and exploitation [by Jews] of native farmers and laborers in those provinces in which the Jews are permitted to reside." The widespread assumption was that the Jews were trouble-makers and, because of their role as money lenders, they were parasites wherever they were found. Alexander I's answer to this apparent situation was to create carrot-and-stick conditions that would encourage the Russianization of the Jews and, indeed, their conversion to Christianity. This was a quasi-assimilationist approach to the problem, aiming at de facto cultural genocide of the Jews in Russian territory; thus the encouragement for Jewish children to attend Russian schools and the withholding of state monies from Jewish schools, as well as the requirement that the Jews use only Russian, German, or Polish in interaction with the state. The 1804 statute also sought the movement of the Jews into occupations from which they would be less "exploitive" of the gentile population; thus, the categories of farmer, manufacturer, and artisan were favored, and those of "merchant and Burgher" were not. On the other hand, the expulsion option was also brought into play, and in some cases Jews were prohibited from living in certain towns and cities. Jews were also prohibited from holding rented property or owning taverns, pubs, or inns. But, if they took up agriculture as an occupation or constructed the "most needed" factories, they would be given temporary tax exemption (Dubnow 1918, 2:166). As noted, Alexander I also sought the conversion of the Jews, and in 1817 he would create a Society of Israelite Christians toward that end.

In 1804, Alexander I also reworked his mother's censorship laws so as to make them more efficient and consistent. He appointed Prince Alexander N. Golitsyn to the post of Minister of Religious

Affairs and People's Education and also made him Russia's chief censor. Golitsyn was a Russian Orthodox zealot and used his position to promote his personal religious views (*Russian History Encyclopedia* 2004). His approach to the Jews leaned toward segregation, for he suspected them of proselytizing. For instance, he presented alleged evidence to this effect to Czar Alexander I, who then forbade Jews from working "in a house service of Christians" in the province of Voronezh (Shumulevich and Kipnis 2005, 2). On the other hand, Golitsyn did have a role in attempting to suppress a number of court trials of Jews falsely accused of blood libel. This directive was often violated, however, sometimes under the direct order of Alexander I (Palomino 1971).

As the nineteenth century progressed, Russian nationalism grew. With it came a growing official concern over the centrifugal forces that minority groups might create if they too were to become nationalistic. Here the Russians had only to look at the pressures that existed in the rival Hapsburg Empire. In 1867, the Austrian Hapsburgs were forced to share power with their Hungarian subjects in what was known thereafter as the Dual Monarchy. The Russian autocracy was looking for ways to avoid this decentralizing possibility. As the historian Ernest Haas puts it, "the answer [the czars came up with] was Russianization." This meant "inducing the minorities to give up their cultures in favor of assimilating into Russian culture by adopting [Russian] Orthodoxy and redefining themselves as part of a primordial-organic collectivity" (Haas 2000, 333). The process went by the term *sliianie* or the "melting of nationalities." Again we have a strategy that aimed at de facto cultural genocide for minority groups. The policy primarily entailed assuring the domination of the Russian language and, in the case of the Jews, minimizing or banning the use of oral and written Hebrew.

Russianization, however, went beyond language. Significantly, Orthodox Christianity was identified as an ideological component of Russian nationalism. Again to quote Haas, the Russian nation was "defined as a collective individual formed by ethnic, primordial factors such as blood and soil, and characterized by an enigmatic soul or spirit. The spirit though innate in the people was really . . . institutionally embodied in the Orthodox faith" (Haas 2000, 330). If the Jewish minority was ever to be truly Russian, its members would have to convert to Russian Orthodox Christianity. It was to this end that the czars practiced policies of both isolation and assimilation when it came to Russia's Jews.

Alexander I was followed by Nicholas I (reigned 1825–1855), a czar who appeared to have a deep emotional commitment to the anti-Semitic assumptions of his culture. Indeed, he lived within the anti-Semitic paradigm every bit as much as the stereotypical Russian or Ukrainian peasant did. During a youthful tour of Russia he wrote in his diary that the Jews were "the ruin of the peasants. . . . Their commercial pursuits drain the strength from the hapless White Russian people. . . . They are regular leeches" (Dubnow 1918, 14). No wonder that when he came to the throne he felt enmity toward the Jews. It was Nicholas I who decreed in 1827 that Jewish boys, starting at age twelve, would be drafted into the Russian army for a twenty-five-year term of service. These were the so-called Cantonist Decrees, and they were designed, at least in part, to remove Jewish boys from their home environment, the better to convert them to Orthodox Christianity (Dubnow 1918, 22ff.). The only way to escape this process was for a Jewish family to bribe government officials or, once again, take up farming. Farming seemed to be one of the government's favored ways of getting the Jews out of businesses that were seen as exploiting the Russian peasants. Special schools for Jewish children were also established. If the Jewish leadership suspected this latter project of seeking to proselytize their children, they were correct. Nicholas I's declaration on the subject stated, "The purpose of education of the Jews is to bring them nearer to the Christians and to uproot their harmful beliefs which are influenced by the Talmud" (Jewish Virtual Library 2011b). Later, under Nicholas's minister of education Count Sergei Uvarov, the intent of the czar would become explicit. In 1840 Uvarov would prepare a "secret set of proposals," the purpose of which was to use educational reforms for "the destruction of the cultural and religious foundation of Russian Judaism" (Edwards 1982, 47). Cultural genocide was Nicholas I's official end game.

The historian Paul Johnson describes this approach to the Jews as "the first modern exercise in social engineering, treating human beings (in this case the Jews) as earth or concrete, to be shoveled around." He suggests that it is a consequence of the Russians seeing the Jews as an "undesirable, semi-criminal community" (Johnson 1987, 358–359). Perhaps; but at this stage the government still considered them capable of being assimilated. It might be noted that Nicholas and his ministers had no particular love for other minorities under Russian rule, either, such as Polish Catholics, Baltic Lutherans, and the Muslims of the Russian steppes. All were to be targets of Nicholas's "official nationalism," which aimed at "socially engineering" all the Russian peoples to blind devotion to "Orthodoxy, Autocracy, and Nationality." Yet the Jews, whose "religious and ethnic traditions departed so radically from the norm" set by Nicholas (Edwards 1982, 45), were destined to be dispossessed and repositioned ("shoveled about") in a particularly harsh and repetitive way.

Nicholas I used the censorship laws he had inherited toward his Russianizing ends. Not only did he want to censor out of existence any Jewish ideas and values but he also looked to banish Western views, which, ever since the Decembrist Revolt by liberal elements of the Russian gentry, he feared were beginning to endanger genuine Russian ideals. And it should be kept in mind that since the Napoleonic era, the Russians had suspected their Jewish subjects of being conduits for just such subversive thinking. In 1826, in the hope of "direct[ing] public opinion into agreeing with present political circumstances and views of the government," the censorship law was expanded to 230 articles (the 1804 version of Alexander I had 46). Soon thereafter, an "ecclesiastical censorship statue" was promulgated, confirming the Russian Orthodox Church's right to ban any text, art, or performance contrary to the precepts of religion (*Russian History Encyclopedia* 2004).

Forced education and censorship can be said to be the two pillars of Nicholas I's "official nationalism." It was really a naive approach to cultural uniformity, for it was as difficult to erase the Jewishness of Russia's Jews as it would have been to uproot the ubiquitous fantasies of anti-Semitism among many of Russia's Greek Orthodox. The dominant thought collectives of both groups ran too deep, and the knowledge each group had of the other too narrowly stereotyped to be reversed in a few generations.

Nicholas I's successor, Alexander II (reigned 1855–1881), was a ruler with a lighter touch. He is seen as a relative liberal because he was the one who finally emancipated the serfs in 1861. It was also under Alexander II that the Cantonist Decrees were repealed and certain categories of Jews, such as medical doctors and "useful merchants," were allowed to live outside the Pale. Jewish populations grew up in St. Petersburg, Moscow, Odessa, and other large cities, and they became active in the professions and intellectual life of the cities. Many historians describe this as a liberal phase in the life of Jews under Russian authority (Johnson 1987, 359). It is probably not the case that Alexander granted this relative reprieve to the Jews for humanitarian reasons. His "liberal" approach was almost certainly pragmatic. He had come to power in the last throes of the Crimean War and had blamed the loss of that struggle on Russia's backwardness. Like Catherine the Great, Alexander II felt that the Jews might help in the process of modernization. Unfortunately, his reformist ideas ran into the same problems as had Catherine's proposals. The deep-seated and pervasive anti-Semitism that existed as a national thought collective meant that a visible growth of a Jewish professional class outside the Pale was enough to trigger an exaggerated reaction among the Russian middle class. Newspaper agitation along the lines of the Jews wanting to create a "state within a state" and thereby dominate Russia became increasingly common (Kniesmeyer and Brecher 1995).

Alexander II's liberal strategy for Russia also meant a relative easing of the censorship laws. On April 6, 1865, a decree was issued aimed at giving "relief and convenience to the national press." This meant that outright censorship by a board of censors was replaced by a warning system that could, by steps, lead to the suspension or closure of a publication that displayed a "dangerous orientation." It should be noted that this change applied only to publications in Moscow and St. Petersburg. Also, short books and pamphlets were not freed from direct censorship because of "their greater potential to do harm" (*Russian History Encyclopedia* 2004). As in the past, no effort was made to censor anti-Semitic sentiments.

In an age lacking scientific polling, one way of getting insight into what appears to be an axiomatic popular anti-Semitism is to look at the sentiments of many of Russia's great nineteenth-century novelists. Alexander Pushkin (1799–1837), who wrote during the reign of Nicholas I, occasionally portrayed the "despised Jew," while Nikolai Gogol (1809–1852), also active during Nicholas I's time, was consistent in his depiction of the Jew in negative terms. Later in the century, Feodor Dostoevsky (1821–1881), whose mature period overlaps the reign of Alexander II, also encouraged hatred of Jews. Dostoevsky refers to Alexander II as "The Great Liberator" of the Russian peasantry. Then he goes on to mimic the sentiments of Nicholas I. He asks the rhetorical question "and who was the first to fall upon them [the liberated peasants] as on a victim?" His answer is the Jews (Dostoevsky [1877] 1995, 337). Dostoevsky goes on to insist that the Russian people "as a whole look upon the Jew ... without preconceived hatred." Yet, he claims, it is "the Jews in many respects who shunned the Russians" and "looked upon them with haughtiness." And then, getting the emotive wind into his sails, he asserts that if the Jew had the opportunity, he would take the Russians and "slaughter them to the last man, to the point of complete extermination." No wonder there is "strong dislike" of the Jews among some Russians, he implies. The Jews have brought it upon themselves (Dostoevsky [1877] 1995, 338). The famous Leo Tolstoy had a much more nuanced view of the matter, though still one that suggested something suspect about the character of Russian Jews. In 1908, in answer to an American reporter's question he said, "If there are any bad traits in the Russian Jews they were called forth by the horrible persecutions to which we subjected them" (*New York Times*, August 9, 1908, SM6).

The outlook of these outstanding Russian writers is a striking example of the power of a thought collective to shape the perception of reality even among those of high literacy and great cultural acumen. When it came to the Jews, it would seem that a man of Dostoevsky's accomplishments had no more accurate knowledge of real Jewry than a Russia Orthodox parish priest. In terms of the description of the mind given by Steven Pinker in chapter 1, he slotted into his culturally determined anti-Semitic mental categories all Russian observations about Jews. Those preformed categories created parameters of what was believable and what was unbelievable about this group. If the Jews were disliked by the Russians, the pictures in his head told him it must be the Jews' fault. Tolstoy, on the other hand, moved by religious pacifism, had equally little doubt that the Russian Jews had "bad traits," but allowed for the possibility that Russian persecution had brought them to the fore.

That anti-Semitism was Russia's normative collective point of view is suggested by the fact that after Alexander II's assassination in 1881, Russian policy toward the Jews quickly returned to its historically oppressive path. This was the work of Alexander II's son and heir Alexander III (1881–1894). Alexander III was a man of minimal education (his elder brother, who unexpectedly died in 1865, was supposed to inherit the throne and therefore got the better education). When it became clear that he was to be the heir apparent, he came under the tutelage of the anti-Semite Konstantin Pobedonostsev, then a professor at Moscow State University. Pobedonostsev would later become a high official in Alexander III's government and eventually director general of the Synod of the Russian Orthodox Church. Pobedonostsev encouraged Alexander III's congenital conservatism (the new czar reimposed strict censorship policies) and instilled in Alexander III the belief that the core of Russian patriotism lay in devotion to the Orthodox Christian creed. This orientation would encourage Alexander to view the Jews under Russian rule as alien and dangerous. In 1889, Alexander wrote that "we must never forget that the Jews have crucified our Master and have shed His precious blood" (Riasanovsky 2000, 395). This is not just one man's (albeit the monarch's) mythical belief. According to reports coming out of the British embassy at this time, "the blood libel is widely believed and propagated in Russia" (Perlmann 1981, 303). The czars, as well as their subjects, dwelled within the anti-Semitic paradigm.

The new czar's anti-Semitism also fed a suspicion that Jews were active in revolutionary groups, including the one that assassinated his father, Alexander II. No doubt there were some idealistic young Jews who were involved in the revolutionary societies of the time, but according to Dubnow only one such activist was actually involved with the group that assassinated the czar. This was a women, Hesia Hoffman, whose residence the assassins used before the attack. It was a function of the prevailing thought collective, which allowed the Jews to be so often used as scapegoats, that her part became exaggerated into an "important role." It was not long before Russian newspapers with connections to the government began to imply that the Jews were behind the assassination of Alexander II. Rumors were then publicized that attacks on provincial Jewish communities were being organized. Deliberately or not, these uncensored actions on the part of the newspapers acted as a self-fulfilling prophecy (Dubnow 1918, 243–244). Soon, Russian territories where Jews resided suffered repeated outbreaks of pogroms, many of which appear to have been officially sanctioned (Dubnow 1918, 247ff.).

A year after taking the throne, Alexander III issued the so-called May Laws. These were "temporary" regulations that ended up lasting for some thirty years, which renewed and extended restrictions on Russia's Jewish population. They initially restricted Jewish residence outside of designated cities and towns, forbade the holding of leases and mortgages beyond those same cities and towns, and made it illegal for Jews to do business on Sunday. Subsequently other restrictions were added. Soon the Jews could not work as lawyers or marry Christians unless they themselves converted to Christianity, and strict quotas were enacted on the number of Jewish students who could enter high schools and universities.

Some, including Alexander Solzhenitsyn, have rationalized that the May Law forbidding Jewish residence outside of the designated cities and towns was, in part, an effort to protect them from violence of pogroms (Devlin 2002, 193). Given Alexander III's religiously fueled hatred of the Jews and his government's complicity in the pogroms, this seems unlikely. Taken together, the May Laws and the pogroms of the late 1880s and 1890s helped initiate a snowballing exodus of Jews from Russian territory, many of whom would end up in the United States.

In November of 1894, Alexander III died of kidney disease at the age of forty-nine. He was succeeded by his ill-fated eldest son, Nicholas II (reigned 1894–1917), who turned out to be the last of the Russian czars. Because his father's death was unexpected, Nicholas's early exposure to government administration was minimal. At the age of twenty-six, he came to the throne having only served as chairman of the Siberian Railway Committee and a member of the State Military Council. Under the circumstances, he decided to follow his father's conservative policies, declaring, "I want everyone to know that I will devote all strength to maintain, for the good of the whole nation, the principle of absolute autocracy, as firmly and as strongly as did my late lamented father" (Radziwill 1931, 100).

Unfortunately for Nicholas II, circumstances would make it impossible to keep this pledge. The years of his reign evolved into ones of social and political breakdown in Russia. As things turned out, this was bad news not just for the czar but also for Russia's Jews, because, as Shlomo Lambroza and John Klier put it, "whenever the social and political fabric threatened to come unraveled—be it through peasant unrest, labor disorders, or anti-revolutionary political activity—the Jews present a weak and poorly defended target, one which the local authorities felt little incentive to protect" (Lambroza and Klier 1998, 193). It could not be otherwise within a culture that had cultivated anti-Semitism for centuries.

In the face of changing historical circumstances Nicholas proved too insular, and perhaps simply not intelligent enough, to meet the resulting challenges of breakdown. The 1904–1905 Russo-Japanese War exposed these flaws in the czar. Despite the loss of both Russian fleets, logistical problems involved in supplying a Russian army 6,000 miles from St. Petersburg along the single-track Trans-Siberian Railroad, repeated defeats in the field, and fiscal problems, Nicholas II could not imagine the possibility of defeat. Indeed, according to the biographer Robert Warth, the czar thought the war was good for the Russian people because it would boost their patriotism (Warth 1997, 67). It took intercession by the czar's mother to get him to agree to peace negotiations.

The 1905 defeat by Japan sparked unrest and revolution. In response, and following the advice of Count Sergei Witte, the relatively progressive president of the Council of Ministers, Nicholas issued the October Manifesto promising civil rights and an elected legislative council (Duma) for the country. The pronouncement came as a surprise both to the people of Russia and to its far-flung bureaucracy, with the result that, at least among government officials, it caused disarray. Part of that disarray was the near-total collapse of the government's censorship apparatus. Witte, having second thoughts about the liberal turn, would complain that "the Manifesto cut Russia's past from its present like a scalpel" (Witte 1990).

Out of this disarray also came an increase in the activity of violent reactionary movements often allied with conservative elements of the government. As we will see below, these reactionary movements would direct much of their wrath toward the Jews, on the premise that they were the disloyal community that allegedly led the revolutionary opposition to the czar. As Witte put it, "violent outbreaks . . . took place all over the country, the reactionary manifestations involving (of course) anti-Jewish pogroms. These last were organized (or at least encouraged) by local authorities" (Witte 1990). The count actually had a reputation of being friendly to the Jews, and when he met Theodor Herzl in St. Petersburg in 1903, he told him that "I personally consider myself a great friend of the Jews" (Frankl 1949, 100). It is true that he had individual friends who were Jewish and had even employed Jews. However, when it came to government policy, his attitude was driven by pragmatism. He once told Alexander III that "if the Jewish question could be solved by dumping all of Russia's Jews into the Black Sea that would be that, but since such a course was not possible the answer must be the gradual lifting of the many legal disabilities under which the Jews labored" (Harcave 2004, 42–43). He repeated this prescription to Herzl in 1903 (Frankl 1949, 100).

Whatever Witte's real opinion and influence, Nicholas II's policies during the first decade of his rule had done nothing to undermine popular belief that the Jews were involved in the unrest shaking the empire. Correspondence from the British embassy in Russia to the Foreign Ministry in London indicated that Nicholas "has a special hatred of the Jews," believing, like his father, that "all that happens to the Jews is deserved because they themselves wanted that the blood of Christ should remain 'upon us and upon our children'" (Perlmann 1981, 300). Thus anti-Semitic persecution had gone on unabated. For instance, in October of 1898 Nicholas had the Jews expelled from Moscow and St. Petersburg, and generally approved of their use as scapegoats. The year 1903 saw the publication of the forged *Protocols of the Elders of Zion* (a text purporting to describe a Jewish plan for achieving global domination), actually written by the Russian secret police. Also on April 6–8 of that year occurred the infamous three-day pogrom at Kishinev, in Bessarabia. This pogrom affords a good example of the power of a skewed information environment saturated with powerful negative emotives to turn an incident (in this case the murder of a Christian child by a relative) into a murderous riot against a feared out-group. The anti-Semitic newspaper *Bessarabian* published the insinuation that the Jews killed the child, and a second paper, the *Light*, described the murder in terms of blood libel—that is, that the child had been killed for his blood in preparation of matzo. The result was forty-seven dead and ninety-seven severely wounded Jewish citizens and seven hundred houses looted and destroyed. The local authorities let the rioting run its course before intervening on the third day.

Come the 1905 revolution, the Jews were assumed to be among the most active participants. Even years later, someone of the stature of Alexsander Solzhenitsyn believed this to be the case (Ericson and Mahoney 2006, 491). Nicholas himself is said to have believed that the Jews played a prominent role in all revolutionary conspiracies. Truth here seemed hardly relevant to the fact that the Jews were destined to be victimized by reactionary elements for the uprising. As Solzhenitsyn puts it, "Angered by the persistent nature of [1905 through 1907] violence . . . the ruling circles in Petersburg were not above yielding to the temptingly simple view that there was nothing organically wrong with Russia and that the entire revolution . . . was a malicious Jewish plot" (Ericson and Mahoney 2006, 495). It is within such an information environment that the "Union of the Russian People," a virulent anti-Semite political party, came into being in 1905 demanding the reinstatement of all of Russia's historical restrictions on the Jews. The party recruited its own "militia" called the Black Hundreds, who proceeded to initiate pogroms and assassinations against "Jews and members of the radical intelligentsia." Nicholas II did nothing to interfere with these activities and was perhaps sympathetic to their cause (*Jewish Virtual Library* 2011a).

So ingrained was Russia's anti-Semitic thought collective that even those who in 1905 rose up against the government also rose up against the Jews. As a consequence, a second pogrom occurred in

Kishniev in 1905, when protests against the Russian government spilled over into attacks on Jews.

Thus, the sudden turn toward liberalism inaugurated by the October Manifesto, which Russia's Jews hoped would lessen their political and civil restrictions, could not rescind centuries of racist indoctrination. In fact, it could only serve to spark a reactionary backlash. As the czar's brother-in-law Alexander Romanov protested, "concessions or new rights to the Jews were unthinkable, that we could not afford to be merciful to a race which the Russian people hate" (qtd. in Atchison 2011).

CONCLUSION

The well-known social scientist Arjun Appadurai has noted that violence against minorities is one common way that dominant groups develop and reinforce their identities (Appadurai 2006, 7). A more brutal way of putting it is to quote Philip Gourevitich (writing about Rwanda), who tells us that "genocide, after all, is an exercise in community-building" (1998, 95). If this is so, then anti-Semitic violence can be seen as one of the primary instruments of Russian nation-building.

Much like the experience of the European colonists operating against the indigenous Indian population of North America, the Russians wavered between physical genocide and cultural genocide. Similarly, moves in the direction of physical genocide were sporadic and unsystematic. One gets massacres (in America) and pogroms (in Russia) instead of centrally organized concentration camps equipped with gas chambers. Attempts at cultural genocide, while conceived in some detail by the czarist government, were never efficiently and effectively carried out. The closest we come to actually enforcing such a strategy is in the infamous Cantonist Decrees of

Nicholas I in 1827. This act essentially took twelve-year-old Jewish boys and placed them in a totalitarian environment for twenty-five years for the purpose of cultural and religious remolding.

The non-Jewish Russian people were, of course also victims of their own historically bred anti-Semitism. It warped their sense of community by creating a "severe pathology" in the heart of their "sacred ideology of nationhood" (Appadurai 2006, 1). Trapped in the natural localness of peasant communities and segregated town and city neighborhoods, they had little or no real knowledge of the Jews, their history in Europe in general and Russia in particular, or their lifestyles and aspirations. All they knew was what the Russian Orthodox Church, the czarist and provincial governments, and the censored official press told them. Centuries of anti-Semitic folklore had created categories in the minds of the majority that precluded the need for investigation and evidence. Insinuation and innuendo, put forth in negatively emotive terms, were sufficient to take any rumor or distorted story and slot it into the mental category of the "parasitic Jew" carried around in the heads of millions of Russians of all classes and all levels of education. Such was the nature of the Russian thought collective when it came to the Jewish people.

4

ISRAEL AND PALESTINIAN
CULTURAL GENOCIDE

Once more the theoretical considerations we have been working with will come into play in our consideration of Israeli policies toward the Palestinians. For, as surely as the Russian czars sought to contain and ultimately destroy Jewish culture within their territories, the same aim is held by the Israeli government (past and present) toward the Palestinians under their control. Israelis, like South African whites before them, like to think of themselves as an isolated Western enclave in the midst of a non-Western world. Yet in both cases, the result of this attitude is not integration with the West but rather a self-imposed isolation that has allowed for the preservation of racist and ethnocentric attitudes bred of outdated imperialism and colonialism—attitudes that the rest of the West seeks to move beyond. As a consequence, Israel has developed a particularly inbred form of natural localness. The vast majority of Israelis have great difficulty in acquiring and/or applying accurate contextual knowledge to the understanding of nonlocal events that nonetheless have direct influence on shaping their perceptions of their local situation. Despite claims of freedom of the press, the popular stylizing of news in Israel allows for the manipulation of attitudes and behaviors, particularly about non-Jews. Such manipulation does, in fact, influence the beliefs and behavior of not only Israeli Jews but also their Zionist supporters worldwide. As usual, the vehicles for this manipulation are the government and managed media and the use of emotive language, as well as the presentation of "expert opinion." The end product of this manipulation is a thought collective that is evolving toward an ever more distorted view of reality.

As we have seen, this same process operated to create the thought collective necessary for the dispossession, segregation, and near extermination of the Native American population, as well as the brutal and discriminatory treatment of Jews in Russia. Now, not without irony, it also has created a vicious thought collective for Israeli Jews and Zionists in general. The result is a Jewish state that has long pursued, and continues to pursue, policies of cultural genocide against its chosen "other."

THE CONCEPT OF TRANSFER: ETHNIC CLEANSING IN THEORY

For much of the nineteenth and early twentieth centuries, the virulent anti-Semitic situation in Russian-controlled territory was not replicated in central and western Europe. Indeed, the path of benign cultural genocide through a process of secularization, inter-marriage, and assimilation seemed open for Jews in countries such as France and Germany, at least through the period of World War I. When one looks at the history of Zionism, the movement that sought to solve the problem of European anti-Semitism through the creation of a Jewish state in Palestine, one finds that the bulk of candidates for the role of Jewish colonial "pioneers" in Palestine were from eastern Europe. That is, these early "pioneers" came from Russian-controlled or -influenced territory, and many of them and their immediate ancestors had suffered the repression described in the last chapter. It was not until the Nazi Party grew influential in the face of Germany's defeat in World War I and the Great Depression of the late 1920s and 1930s that things changed radically for the Jews of central, and eventually western, Europe. At that point they too would seek to escape from a virulent anti-Semitism that sought the physical genocide of the Jews. Finding escape to places like the United States and Great Britain increasingly difficult, many would end up in Palestine.

Settlement in Palestine created a new situation for Europe's Jews. Coming from an arena of persecution, they now stepped into an arena where they exercised privilege, particularly after Great Britain took charge of Palestine following the collapse of the Ottoman Empire. In some ways the position of the Zionist settlers resembled that of the colonists in North America examined in chapter 2. Both those earlier European settlers and the Zionist "pioneers" in Palestine were beneficiaries of European imperialism. Both groups took with them an inculcated Western racism and chauvinism that also characterized European behavior throughout its history of imperial and colonial expansion. Indeed, American Zionists in the early 1920s compared the Palestinians to hostile American Indians and themselves to American pioneers bringing civilization to the wilderness (Davidson 2001, 46). This being the case, just how tolerant would the victims of religious persecution really be toward the native peoples they encountered in their respective "promised lands"? We have already seen the answer when it came to the Puritans and others in North America.

So it was that the Zionist movement came to shape its cause within a certain mind-set. Its membership saw themselves as a persecuted minority, but also as Europeans. Therefore, even while they hated and feared those who discriminated against them, they had inculcated within their own cultural outlook a similar sense of racial and cultural superiority that would allow them to discriminate against non-Europeans. It was a complex psychological position to be in.

The Zionists eventually developed a strong organization with a single-minded focus on Palestine. When it came to that land, the Zionist reference points were all self-centered. That is, they were creating a closed information environment wherein they spoke exclusively of their own needs and "rights" almost solely to themselves and those who supported them. They lacked vital contextual knowledge of the actual situation relevant to the indigenous population, its history, culture, and present aspirations. Nor, as an organization, did the Zionist movement seek such information out. Thus their decision-making process was bound to be flawed. Their leaders would later admit that they thought little about the possibility of indigenous resistance. As the Zionist leader and first president of Hebrew University Judah Magnes put it, "We seem to have thought of everything, except the Arabs" (Lilienthal 1979, 150). When they considered the Palestinians at all, it was through a prevailing Western stereotype that pictured them as a primitive folk who could be bought off.

The initial Zionist answer to this question of how tolerant they would eventually be toward the native people of Palestine was offered by the founder of modern Zionism, Theodor Herzl. On June 12, 1895, he wrote in his diary: "We must expropriate gently, the private property. . . . We shall try to spirit the penniless population across the border by procuring employment for it in the transit countries whilst denying it any employment in our own country" (Zohn 1960, 1: 88). Though he almost certainly did not think of it this way, by taking this position the founder of the Zionist movement prescribed something like a Pale of Settlement for non-Jews in order to pave the way for a purely Jewish state. It should be noted that at this time Herzl was unsure just where that state would be located. He felt Argentina was a possible venue, and later would entertain the prospect of Uganda. He therefore does not specify who the "expropriated" might be. Regardless, Herzl knew that expropriation was a generic behavior for colonists during the eras of European imperial dominance and, wherever the Jewish state might be realized, he expected it to be ethnically cleansed of non-Jews. And, of course, to the extent that culture is rooted in geography— in one's traditional and ancestral place—such ethnic cleansing constitutes cultural genocide. As it turned out, his mostly eastern European supporters would not seriously consider any locale other than Palestine. Herzl was not a violent man and imagined that this ethnic cleansing could be engineered solely through the manipulation of the economy, but those who came after him would not be so delicate.

After his death in 1904, leadership of the World Zionist Organization eventually passed to Chaim Weizmann. Born in Russia in 1874, Weizmann immigrated to England in 1904. There he worked as a chemist and, in that capacity, made notable contributions to the British war effort during World War I. These achievements brought him to the attention of British media and political leaders, and he used those growing contacts to help convince Britain's wartime government to issue the Balfour Declaration in 1917.

At first Weizmann took a position against the ethnic cleansing of Palestinians. We can surmise that, as he was personally familiar with Russian policies toward the Jews, approximating the same policies by Jews toward Palestinians initially created too much cognitive dissonance for him. Speaking to a Zionist conference in London in September of 1919, he declared that "we who have been driven out ourselves cannot drive out others. We shall be the last people to drive off the Fellah [peasant] from his land. . . . The Arabs will live among us; they won't suffer; they will live among us as Jews do here in England. This is our attitude towards the Arabs. Any other attitude is criminal" (Simons 2003, 1).

As well intentioned as this may have been (we will give Weizmann the benefit of the doubt this time), his fellow Zionists did not act on this principle. When they entered Palestine in the baggage train of the British army, which served as a vehicle for the expansion of empire, they did not seriously factor the native people into their plans. They went about creating an exclusively Jewish economy, which, when it employed Arabs at all, did so as cheap labor. The Zionists also required the eviction of all Palestinian residents from the land they purchased (thus giving the lie to Weizmann's statement about the Fellah and the land). This means that the Zionists never believed (and still do not) that the local population had any legitimate claims to Palestine. We know what those claims were because they are documented by the ill-fated American King-Crane Commission. In 1919, that commission determined that the peoples of Greater Syria, of which Palestine was a part, wanted self-determination within an independent greater Arab state promised by the British to Sharif Hussein of Mecca in exchange for his willingness to rebel against the Ottoman Empire. That promise was never fulfilled. Under the circumstances, it meant little to the Palestinians if Weizmann had an initial inclination to treat them as good neighbors. They had been betrayed by Weizmann's patrons and co-conspirators and, as suggested above, the incoming Zionists proved in fact to be quite bad neighbors (Pappe 2004, 72–116). All of this happened within the environment of Europe's imperialist thought collective.

As it turned out, what the British and the Zionists got from the locals was evolving resistance to their imperial and colonial occupation. There were anticolonial demonstrations as early as 1922, and in

1929 a large rebellion took place, in the course of which hundreds of lives were lost. It is over this ten-year period of growing resistance that Weizmann reversed this position. If you will, his career as a Zionist now demanded compliance with the evolving Zionist variant of the imperialist thought collective. In 1919 there may have been some psychological contradiction between the demands of this new Zionist vision and the treatment the Jews themselves had received in Russia. For Weizmann, however, the contradiction was gone by 1929. In any case, the ideological rigidity of the Zionist position, with its uncompromising ultimate goal of an exclusively Jewish state, made it impossible to negotiate with the Palestinians the sort of accommodations that might have made Weizmann's initial position of intergroup friendship possible. What indigenous natural resistance to imperialism meant to Weizmann and many other Zionists was that the Palestinians could now be envisioned as enemies and anti-Semites and therefore could be legitimately expelled from the future Jewish state. And so "we shall be the last people to drive off the Fellah from his land" quickly transformed itself into a number of population-transfer proposals. Indeed, "transfer" now became the polite term for proposed ethnic cleansing and cultural genocide.

There was at this time a recent precedent for the application of the concept of transfer. In 1923, as ethnic Greeks fled western Turkey with retreating Greek armies, Greece and Turkey signed the "Convention Concerning the Exchange of Greek and Turkish Populations." Eventually, some two million people were uprooted by this agreement. It allowed for compulsory denial of citizenship to ethnic Greeks in Turkey and ethnic Turks in Greece and the subsequent deportation of those who did not leave voluntarily.

Another immediate impetus to the notion of transfer was the British decision to sever Transjordan from Palestine proper. This was done in 1922 so as to provide a territory for Abdullah, the older son of Sharif Hussein of Mecca. If the Arabs were not to get their large and independent Arab state, the British were willing to give Hussein's sons positions as rulers of small British client states. Thus, Hussein's son Feisal would become king of Iraq and Abdullah, the emir of Jordan. Dividing Transjordan from Palestine irked the Zionists (who were not allowed to settle there), some of whom, even today, feel that Jordan was "stolen" from them. However, Weizmann seized on the separation to propose that the Palestinians living to the west of the Jordan River be transferred to Transjordan. "Surely, if we cannot cross the Jordan the Arabs could," he wrote to the British Colonial Secretary Lord Passfield, in 1930 (Weizmann 1983, 591–592). On November 1 of that same year, he publicly proposed transfer of landless Palestinians to Transjordan in an article published in the *Week End Review* (Weizmann 1983, 605–606). At later moments, when the Zionists renewed their hope that Transjordan would become part of the future Jewish state, the concept of transfer of Palestinians was directed toward Iraq and Syria.

The Zionists subsequently applied pressure to the British government to consider a transfer plan, linking it to the success of the partition plan put forth by the 1937 Peel Commission. There is some evidence that the British were willing to go along with this idea and indeed, at a meeting between Weizmann, David Ben Gurion, and Colonial Secretary Ormsby-Gore on June 28, 1937, the last agreed that "the Arabs in the Jewish part [of Palestine] would have to be transferred" (Simons 2003, subsection on Weizmann, 8). As the probable outbreak of World War II became clearer to British leaders, they retreated from their advocacy of partition in order to keep the goodwill of the Arabs. But Weizmann never ceased to promote the possibility of transfer (Weizmann 1942, 337).

Weizmann was by no means alone in pressing for the ethnic cleansing of Palestinians. His fellow Zionist leader and sometimes rival Ben Gurion also promoted the transfer of Arabs. Actually, he seems to have paralleled Weizmann's evolutionary path. In 1918 Ben Gurion, like Weizmann, was against the idea of transfer. He published an article in Hebrew entitled "The Rights of Jews and Others in Palestine" in which he wrote, "Under no condition may we harm the rights of these inhabitants [the Arabs]. . . . It is not proper nor possible to deport the country's present inhabitants" (Simons 2003, subsection on Ben Gurion, 10). By the 1930s, and probably earlier, he had changed his tune. In a July 9, 1936, meeting with Sir Arthur Wauchope, the British high commissioner in Palestine, Ben Gurion argued for the deportation of landless Palestinian peasants to Transjordan. He used almost the same words as did Weizmann. He told Wauchope that if Transjordan is closed to the Jews, "it surely cannot be closed to the Arabs." Ben Gurion's associate, Moshe Shertok, was also at the meeting and assured the high commissioner that the Zionists would "gladly spend . . . money to settle the displaced Arabs in Transjordan" (Simons 2003, subsection on Ben Gurion, 1). A year later, in 1937, Ben Gurion was still pushing for transfer, now adding Syria to Transjordan as a possible area of relocation (Simons 2003, subsection on Ben Gurion, 2).

As Ben Gurion pursued this idea, it expanded in his mind. In July 1937 he wrote in his diary, "it would be of tremendous advantage to us . . . for every transferred Arab, one could settle four Jews on the land." He was soon ready to see transfer forcefully imposed upon the Palestinian Arabs. In a 1941 memorandum, he noted that "complete transfer without compulsion—and ruthless compulsion at that—is hardly imaginable" (Simons 2003, subsection on Ben Gurion, 8). For Ben Gurion, compulsory transfer of as many Arabs as possible was now a necessary step toward achieving "a truly

Jewish state." He doubted if the British had the "courage" to take up such a project. However, he was determined that the Zionists would do so the moment they got the chance. "Any wavering on our part as to the necessity of this transfer, any doubt on our part as to the possibility of its achievement, any hesitation on our part as to the justice of it, are likely to lose us a historic opportunity which will not reoccur" (Simons 2003, subsection on Ben Gurion, 3–4). Ben Gurion's hoped-for moment would come late in the year 1947 and throughout 1948.

Both Weizmann and Ben Gurion, as well as most of the Zionist leadership in Palestine, were now prisoners of a thought collective that restricted reality to the needs of their group. That group, the Ashkenazi Jews, were for the Zionists an "imagined community" that filled their minds to the exclusion of all others, unless those others, like the British, could serve the ends of the dominant thought collective. By 1929, as Weizmann and Ben Gurion looked out onto the world, all incoming data became the equivalent of stylized news, interpreted by their own "experts." We must here keep in mind Daniel Willingham's comment on the difficulty of critical thinking: "the processes of thinking are intertwined with the content of thought" (Willingham 2007, 8–19). For Weizmann and Ben Gurion, the "content of thought" was ideologically restricted. Their Zionism so distorted their perceptions of the world that it became one of Arjun Appadurai's "severe pathologies" that pervert our "sacred ideologies of nationhood" (Appadurai 2006, 1).

ISRAEL'S "WAR OF INDEPENDENCE": ETHNIC CLEANSING IN PRACTICE

In February of 1947 the British government decided to give up its Mandate and leave Palestine. The date for departure was set as

May 15, 1948. Ben Gurion, sensing as early as 1946 that the British could not hold on for long, had been working on contingency plans for taking over Palestine once the British were gone. These efforts culminated in two plans known as Plan Gimel or Plan C and Plan Dalet or Plan D. Gimel or C was a preplanned series of responses to Palestinian resistance to the Zionist presence in Palestine and included the murder of the Palestinian political and military leadership, financial supporters, and destruction of civilian infrastructure. Dalet or D was designed to realize the "systematic and total expulsion" of Palestinians "from their homeland" (Pappe 2007, 28) as a consequence of the upcoming military struggle with the Arabs.

This was, of course, not the public position of the Zionist leadership. That position emphasized mass immigration of Jews into Palestine. But Ben Gurion, Weizmann, and the other Zionist leaders in Palestine knew that that would not be enough to give the Jews a majority in the country. After all, in 1947 there were some one million Palestinians in the territory the Zionists hoped to conquer. Against that number there were 600,000 Jews. For Ben Gurion an acceptable, positive "demographic balance" required at least an 80 percent Jewish majority (Pappe 2007, 48). For that to be achieved Jewish immigration had to be complemented by Arab emigration.

The steps taken in this process of ethnic cleansing have been laid out in detail by the Israeli historian Ilan Pappe. Putting his recounting together with other information, we get the following narrative. David Ben Gurion and the Zionist leadership saw the disintegration of British rule, together with the UN partition plan, as the "unique historical opportunity" they had been hoping for since the 1930s. This was their moment to create an "exclusively Jewish state" and, as Ben Gurion had written back in 1941, there must be no wavering or hesitation in doing what was necessary to rid the country of as many

Arabs as possible. At this point "the country" meant, for the Zionist leadership, all of Palestine west of the Jordan River. They gave up the ambition of conquering Transjordan because they were negotiating a deal with Emir Abdullah (whose army was the most formidable Arab military force in the region) that would assure his staying out of the upcoming war. So even before the end of the Mandate, the Zionists had decided to destroy the UN-promised Palestinian state.

In December of 1947, Palestinian Arabs protested the United Nations plan to partition their country with a three-day general strike and demonstrations. The demonstrations spilled over into assaults on some Jewish shops and markets. Even though these actions were short lived and there was soon a clear indication of a return to "normalcy," Ben Gurion used the incidents as an excuse to trigger Plan Gimel, and subsequent attacks on Palestinian villages and neighborhoods were severe enough to cause some 75,000 Arab residents to run for their lives (Pappe 2007, 40).

When in early January 1948 the first units of an all-volunteer Arab irregular force entered Palestine, the Zionists leadership initiated Plan Dalet (officially inaugurated in March but really acted upon earlier), and ethnic cleansing became a primary military objective. Ben Gurion told his followers that the Arabs were now a "fifth column" and therefore they had to be arrested en masse or expelled. He concluded that "it is better to expel them" (Pappe 2007, 49). And how was one to expel them? Urban areas as well as villages were targeted for violent assaults, and massacres were apparently committed purposefully so as to spread panic among the Arabs of Palestine. Ben Gurion describes the tactics in a diary entry of January 1, 1948. Actions must be "strong and brutal." They must be carried out "without mercy, women and children included." And, finally, "there is no need to distinguish between guilty and not guilty" (Pappe 2007, 69). The Zionist leadership was particularly anxious to destroy a long-standing tradition of Jewish and Arab worker cooperation in Haifa, and the unwritten truce between the Jewish city of Tel Aviv and the Arab town of Jaffa, or anywhere else where Jewish-Arab amity existed (Pappe 2007, 58, 65). By the end of April, some 250,000 Arabs had fled (Pappe 2007, 40). It is to be noted that this was before the entrance of regular Arab military forces into Palestine.

This was, of course, only the beginning. The Zionist "war of independence" went on into early 1949, and a part of it continued to be waged against the unarmed civilian Arab population of Palestine. The Israel historian Benny Morris has described the results: "The principal cause of the mass flight [of Palestinians] . . . was Jewish military attack. Almost every instance—the exodus . . . was the direct and immediate result of an attack on and conquest of Arab neighborhoods and towns" (Morris 1999, 255). Some 419 Arab villages and towns were eventually destroyed and their populations killed or evicted. The details of this process of violent ethnic cleansing have been detailed by Pappe, Nur Masalha, and Benny Morris. When it was all over, Ben Gurion had gotten his "positive demographic balance" and a vast majority of Palestine's Arabs were refugees. Only about 150,000 Arabs remained in what was now Israel. This is what the Arabs call the Nakbah, or "Disaster." Though Weizmann and Ben Gurion certainly did not think of it in this way, one can see the process of ethnic cleansing as the Zionists' answer to the "Holocaust" syndrome of the Jews.

MOVING ON TO CULTURAL GENOCIDE

Having "won" independence, the Israelis embarked upon an ongoing process to "Hebraize" the land they now called their own. Making the land "Hebrew" automatically meant making it no longer Arab. As much as possible of the heritage of Arab culture, like the Arabs themselves, had to be evicted.

This began with a process of renaming things. It turned out that the Zionists had created a "naming committee" back in the 1920s that had the job of "Hebraizing" the small areas of Palestine purchased by the Jewish National Fund (JNF). In 1949, this committee became a subdivision of the JNF and, with the help of archaeologists, geographers, and biblical scholars, began to systematically erase Palestine's Arab history and heritage from Israel's own official records, maps, histories, and so on. This is a process that continues to this day. For instance, in July of 2009 Israel's Transport Ministry announced that road signs (which now appear in Hebrew, Arabic, and English) would be replaced with signs in Hebrew only. This would happen despite the fact that 20 percent of the population are Arabic speakers and Arabic is supposedly one of Israel's "official languages." The transport minister, Yisrael Katz, asserted that he would not allow pre-1948 names on road signs. Doing so would threaten to turn "Jewish Jerusalem into Palestinian Al-Quds" (BBC 2009).

Also in 1949, an Israeli metanarrative was spun to the effect that when the Zionists arrived, Palestine had a small number of hostile, backward, and nomadic residents but was otherwise largely empty. Thus, according to the history officially taught to all Israelis, and all Jewish children enrolled in Hebrew schools the world over, the only cultural heritage to exist in Israel, past and present, is the Jewish one. To make this alternate history plausible, the Israelis set about destroying many Palestinian archaeological sites and artifacts, ancient mosques, historic houses, and the like, to the extent that UNESCO's World Heritage office describes their actions as "crimes against the cultural heritage of mankind" (Chamberlain 2005). This process is documented in a book by Raz Kletter entitled *Just Past? The Making of Israeli Archeology (2005)*. Through the 1950s, the

Israeli government allowed both Christian and Muslim holy sites, museums, and archives to be looted by their own soldiers and then proceeded to destroy them. Those few Israeli archaeologists who objected were lied to about what was happening (they were told that the Arabs were doing it) and then, if they persisted in their opposition, forced to resign. David Ben Gurion, Moshe Dayan, and Golda Meir were all directly involved in this process of cultural destruction (Rapoport 2008). The process of preventing any public reemergence of Palestinian culture goes on to the present day. For instance, in 2009 UNESCO chose East Jerusalem as the 2009 Arab Capital of Culture. The Israeli government immediately declared that no celebrations or demonstrations to this effect would be allowed. They banned all of the UNESCO-sponsored events not only in Jerusalem but also elsewhere, such as in the city of Nazareth. Parallel Palestinian sports events, a literary festival, and a women's festival were also banned. Presently, Palestinians on the West Bank are under some fifteen hundred military regulations, many of which attack their ability to express themselves culturally and politically. Thus, Military Order 938 makes it illegal to hold a Palestinian flag or listen to patriotic Palestinian music (*Palestine Monitor* 2009).

It should come as no surprise that Israeli textbooks mention none of this, but rather, according to Professor Daniel Bar-Tal of Tel Aviv University, "present the view that Jews are involved in a justified, and even humanitarian, war against an Arab enemy that refuses to accept and acknowledge the existence and rights of Jews in Israel." He found that from the beginning of the state of Israel up to the present time, Israeli schoolbooks defamed Arabs by labeling them as "killers" and "robbers." Israeli Jews, on the other hand are consistently pictured as "improving the country in ways they believe the Arabs are incapable of" (Meehan 1999, 19). Jamal Atamneh, coordinator of the Arab Education Committee in Support of Local

Councils, a Haifa-based NGO, notes that although the textbooks
used by the Arab Israeli population are written in Arabic, they are
not prepared by Palestinians, who also have no advisory role in
their preparation. "For the past 15 years, not one new Palestinian
academic has been placed in a high position in the [Education]
Ministry. There are no Palestinians involved in preparing the
Arabic-language curriculum [and] obviously, there is no such thing
as affirmative action in Israel" (Meehan 1999, 20). As As'ad Ghanem
of Haifa University notes, Israeli Arab education budgets are considerably lower than those of the Israeli Jewish sector, and this
is a consequence of "continuing discrimination in practically every
sphere of life" (Ghanem 2001, 159). One consequence of these
cumulative efforts has been to make "Nakbah denial" easier for
Israeli Jews and Zionists generally. As far as Palestinians are concerned, Nakbah denial is the Israeli version of Holocaust denial.

After 1948, some of the destroyed villages of the Arabs were transformed into Israeli towns. In a rare moment of public truthfulness,
the Israeli general and politician Moshe Dayan stated, "Jewish villages were built in the place of Arab villages. You do not even know
the names of these Arab villages, and I do not blame you because
geography books [naming them] no longer exist. . . . There is not
one single place built in this country that did not have a former Arab
population" (Lis and Khoury, April 4, 2009). As to Dayan's reference to missing geography books, in January of 2010 the Al Jazeera
news network reported on an interview conducted with an Israeli
citizen doing a doctoral thesis at Ben Gurion University. The student's research shows that Israeli forces "plundered and destroyed
tens of thousands of Palestine books in the years after the State's
establishment." According to the researcher, this was done "in the
framework of its plan to Judaize the country and cut off its Arab residents from their nation and culture." It was a "cultural massacre,"

concludes this researcher (Al Jazeera January 1, 2010). Over the intervening years there have been periodic attacks on Palestinian libraries and archives, not only in Israel and the Occupied Territories but also in other countries such as Lebanon. These actions did not go unnoticed. In the summer of 2002, the American Library Association issued a resolution stating that the organization (which has 450,000 members) "deplores the destruction of library and cultural resources anywhere in the world, and therefore the destruction of these Palestinian library and cultural resources." The resolution was considerably watered down under pressure. Its original version directly named the Israeli government as the perpetrator of the destruction (Heuer 1999).

Where the destroyed villages were not transformed into Israeli places, their ruins were bulldozed away and forests were planted in their place. Ilan Pappe tells us that this was part of what Israel calls "making the desert bloom." Referring to the Web page of the Jewish National Fund, Pappe notes that many of the largest and most popular forest areas promoted by the site were not, as the JNF claims, built upon "arid and desert-like areas" but on top of the ruins of once thriving Palestinian towns. Pappe refers to this as the "deliberate airbrushing of history" (Pappe 2007, 229–234).

To these efforts one can add the destruction and desecration of Palestinian cemeteries, the purposeful uprooting or burning of the crops (particularly olive trees) of Palestinian farmers, the targeting of cultural centers, including the destruction of the Palestinian Ministry of Culture in 2002, and the special attention the Israeli government gave to undermining the Arabs of East Jerusalem following the 1967 war. For instance, the foundations of Jerusalem's Al Aqsa Mosque, one of the most sacred shrines of Islam and the religious and cultural symbol of Palestine, have been physically weakened by twenty-five adjacent Israeli archaeological excavations.

The mosque itself has been the target of repeated acts of terrorism by Israelis, including arson and vandalism. A fanatical sect within Zionism seeks the mosque's total destruction so as to pave the way for the rebuilding of Solomon's temple. This effort is financially funded by Christian fundamentalists, most of whom are Americans (Chehata 2010, 10). Looking back on all this, an Arab Israeli member of the Knesset, Mohammad Barakeh, characterized the Israeli government as an enemy of Palestinian culture (*Haaretz*, April 3, 2009). There is no reason to doubt the truth of Barakeh's statement.

THE CULTURAL IMPOVERISHMENT OF ISRAELI-ARABS

After 1948, in those areas where there were no more Arabs, it was relatively easy to perform cultural genocide. However, as mentioned, there was a remnant of approximately 150,000 Arabs still left in what was now Israel. The Israelis often referred to them as "present absentees" because, even though they had remained in Israel, they often ended up dispossessed of their land and homes. The historian Mark Tessler calls these people "internal refugees." Tessler tells us that the result was that they were "divorced from their traditional social and economic institutional connections," and "cut off from their families and countrymen who resided in states with which Israel remained at war" (Tessler 1994, 281). Both their physical and cultural presence in the Jewish state was seen as threat by the Zionist leadership who, following Ben Gurion's lead, continued to perceive this group as a "fifth column." And so, in October 1948, they were all placed under a system of martial law that lasted until 1966.

What martial law meant for the remaining Palestinians was a regime of restricted travel, curfews, administrative detentions, expulsions, confinement to certain geographical areas, limitation on the freedoms of expression and the press, assembly, and due process. The only legal right left to the Israeli Arabs was the right to vote (they were given Israeli citizenship). Why give a feared and hated minority such a right? According to Ilan Pappe, "it is impossible to miss the irony in the fact that the raw instinct for vote gathering was allowed to overshadow the principal issue of full apartheid" (Pappe 2004, 159). In other words, the reason the Israeli Arabs were left the right to vote is because the various Zionist political parties felt they could capture that vote and thus turn it to their political advantage.

The military regime under which these people were placed facilitated the dispossession, Tessler notes. A systematic transfer of the landed property from the remaining Arabs to Jewish control now took place. This was done by the office of the Custodian of Absentee Property. According to the custodian, any non-Jew who was "absent" from his usual place of residence on or after November 29, 1947, could have his property confiscated. This was so even if you returned home on November 30! (Smith 1988, 154). It was deemed that the bulk of Israel's remaining Arabs were so absent.

The consequences of this process were economically devastating. For instance, the Palestinian Muslim societal structure, with its traditional hierarchy, its public and private endowments, social and economic support systems, and so on, all disappeared. The Palestine Christian community fared little better. Pauperized and isolated, the Palestinians of Israel quickly had the highest unemployment in the country. Mostly rural folk, many were forced to move to urban areas allotted to the Arab community, where they became a classic cheap labor force. The Jewish state proceeded to deny them any personal benefits given to Israeli Jews, they were denied access to over 70 percent of the economy (through the ploy of not having served in the Israeli army), their education budgets were kept to a minimum, and any expression of Palestinian national feelings was made criminal (Pappe 2004, 160).

As Pappe tells us, the only cultural leaders left to this community were the poets. "Poetry was the one area in which national identity survived the Nakbah unscathed. What political activists did not dare express, poets sang out with force" (Pappe 2004, 158). Poetry was the ancient Arab art of choice and it proved able to survive even this Israeli effort of cultural genocide.

A Comparison with the Russian Jewish Experience

It is impossible to review this history without noticing how it overlaps with the treatment of the Jews in czarist Russia examined in the last chapter. For instance, consider the following:

1. Russian anti-Semites saw Jews as Christ killers and a form of ethnic and cultural polluters within a purer Russian and Christian Orthodox body politic. Just so many Israeli Jews see Arab Israelis as would be destroyers of the state of Israel and thus an unwanted deadly force within the Israeli body politic. Moshe Smilansky, a Zionist writer and labor leader, once said of the Palestinian Arabs, "We must not forget that we are dealing with a semi-savage people, which has extremely primitive concepts. . . . There developed among the Arabs base values . . . to lie, to cheat, to harbor grave suspicions and to tell tales . . . and a hidden hatred of the Jews" (Morris 1999, 43–44).

2. Russia's anti-Semitic government under the czars confined the Jews to a small number of specialized job categories. Israeli Jewish society manages to keep Israeli Arabs out of 70 percent of the country's economy.

3. The czarist government of Russia kept the Jews confined to defined geographic areas (the Pale) and otherwise essentially ghettoized them. Israel has restricted the living space of both Arab Israelis and those in the Occupied Territories through the use of zoning regulations, house demolitions, travel restrictions, checkpoints, and the designation of "Jewish only" zones, towns, and cities. On a visit to Italy, ex-Israeli Prime Minister Ariel Sharon explained to Italian Prime Minister Massimo D'Alema that when it came to the Palestinians, the South African "Bantustan model was the most appropriate solution to the conflict" (Eldar 2003).

4. Czarist Russia used extensive censorship and media control to propagate anti-Semitic ideas and accusations. The Israeli government maintains censorship through a military censorship law, and the Israeli politicians and media analysts promote derogatory attitudes and discriminatory policies against Palestinians as necessary for state security. For example, ex-Prime Minister Yitzak Shamir equated the Palestinians to grasshoppers that must be crushed (*New York Times*, April 1, 1988), and ex-Prime Minister Ehud Barak declared that "the Palestinians are like crocodiles, the more you give them meat, the more they want" (*Jerusalem Post*, August 30, 2000). Palestinian violence, even if exercised in resistance to colonial oppression, is typically labeled terrorism.

5. As a result of prolonged propaganda and cultural antipathy, nineteenth- and early twentieth-century Russia eventually produced anti-Semitic political parties, such as the Union of the Russian People, that encouraged violence and pogroms against the Jewish population. By the 1990s

Israel had produced specifically anti-Palestinian political parties such as the Kach movement (Kahane Chai), whose members would periodically wage campaigns of violence against the Palestinian population. In 1993, Kach carried out several attacks on Palestinians in the West Bank, killing four and wounding two. In 1994 Baruch Goldstein, an Israeli-American and supporter of Kach, entered the Ibrahimi Mosque in Hebron and killed twenty-nine Palestinian worshipers.

We should not be too surprised at these parallels. Much the same similarities would evolve in almost every situation where there is a long-term history of consistent public cultivation of hatred and discrimination against a specific minority. On the other hand, there are differences between the policies of czarist Russia and the situation in present-day Israel. Throughout the nineteenth century, there were periodic attempts at the assimilation of the Jews (and other minorities) into the Russian body politic. These were brutal, such as the forced conscription of Jewish youth, and involved the coercive attempt to convert Jews to Russian Orthodox Christianity. There is absolutely no desire on the part of the Israeli government to attempt the conversion and integration of the Palestinians.

CONCLUSION: WHY DO THE ISRAELI JEWS DO THIS?

Individuals subject to prolonged high levels of stress can develop abnormal patterns of behavior. Perhaps this can happen to whole groups of people. If it can, the European Jews are certainly candidates for such a syndrome. The American Israeli peace activist Jeffrey Halpern, in a public talk given in the spring of 2010, explained that most Israeli Jews view themselves as victims. That victimization began centuries ago with the creation of anti-Semitism in Christian

Europe and reached its peak in the Nazi Holocaust. The Nazis were defeated in World War II and European anti-Semitism finally waned. But for the Jews it did not end there. Halpern explained that, with all the European persecutors gone, the Jews refashioned them in the form of the Arabs. So, in Halpern's view, the Zionists brought more than just a European imperialist outlook with them to Palestine. They also brought a deeply ingrained conviction of victimhood that translated any resistance to their colonial ambitions into renewed anti-Semitism. This being the case, the Zionists see their actions in Palestine, the ethnic cleansing and cultural genocide, simply as acts of self-defense against an insidious enemy who hates Jews.

Halpren's explanation gives an added pathological dimension to the Zionist thought collective. In this case it is not just that the Israeli Jews, living under conditions of natural localness, swim in a sea of consistently manipulated news across the media spectrum. It is not just that their thought collective takes on added strength from the fact that most people shape their opinions to coincide with those around them; that people want to fit into their community, and sharing outlooks is an important aspect of this bonding; that once the shared perspective is in place, there is a natural tendency to reinforce it by seeking out information that supports it and ignoring or downplaying that which does not. It is not just that this has resulted in a community-wide point of view underpinning Benedict Anderson's "striking . . . imaginings of fraternity" (Anderson 1991, 203). But it is also that the feelings upon which this thought collective rests are ancient and brooding—a seemingly unchanging and irrefutable worldview. And these almost timeless feelings of victimization really know no national boundaries but pervade a kinship circle that is worldwide. This psychological situation has blinded the Israeli Jewish population and its diaspora backers to their role as persecutors and transposed their victims into symbols of all anti-Semitic enemies of the past.

Whether this explanation has real merit or not, there is no denying the great irony of Zionist behavior. In setting out to save their own cultural heritage, which so many others have sought to destroy in a genocidal fashion, they are in the process of committing cultural genocide against the Palestinians. It seems the cruelest of fates for both sides.

5

THE CHINESE
ASSIMILATION OF TIBET

As was the case in the previous examinations, we are here dealing with two centers of localness: the ancient and very traditional local reality of Tibet, the core of which is Tibetan Buddhism, and the evolving and dynamic culture of the People's Republic of China, the core of which is the customized ideology of Chinese communism. As we will see, the conquest of modern Tibet by the Chinese led to a period of experimentation as the authorities in Beijing sought the most effective and efficient way to assimilate the Tibetans into the Chinese nation. In this effort the Chinese government had all the advantages that come with control of the information environment. For example, Tibetan mass media became an extension of Chinese mass media.

We will also see that the Chinese convinced themselves through a reinterpretation of history that Tibet was always part of China. The Tibetans, on the other hand, found that their traditional ways of life and oral and written histories confirmed an independent past. Thus Chinese occupation of Tibet is not only a struggle to control territory. It is also a struggle to obliterate a cultural past as a basis for present resistance. For this to be accomplished, the Chinese Communist Party (CCP) must not only maintain a supportive thought collective among the Chinese but also remake the thought collective of the Tibetans. They have determined that this can only be done with the destruction of traditional Tibetan religion and its replacement with a patriotic devotion to the Chinese communist way of life.

This process of cultural genocide is accompanied by a storyline designed for Chinese as well as Tibetan consumption. Just as was the case for the settlers on the American frontier relative to the Indians, the Russian public relative to the Jews, and the Israeli Jews relative to the Palestinians, the stronger party must create a thought collective that makes the victims' culture appear antiquated and unworthy of survival. In the past three cases, religion has played an important supporting role in the thought collective of the aggressor. In the case of the Chinese, the denigration of religion as a false ideology and a barrier to progress is an important part of the communist rationale.

It is a function of natural localness that the vast majority of Chinese, be they of the majority Han culture or other various ethnic minorities, know nothing about Tibet, past or present. They will not pay attention to happenings in Tibet unless they reside so close to this far-away place that it is regarded to be "in the neighborhood." Likewise, some will pay attention to the goings on in Tibet if they have friends or relatives there. But in neither case does this include the vast majority of citizens in the People's Republic. This means that the pictures in the heads of this majority will perforce be secondhand and filtered by a very extensive bureaucracy. The capacity of this organization to create and maintain specific messages about the "other" is much greater than the case of the American colonists or the czarist Russians. The Chinese capacity in this regard is comparable to that of the Israeli Zionists.

Thus there is no objectively accurate knowledge of Tibet to be had among the ordinary Chinese or—and this is of greater import—the soldiers of the People's Liberation Army sent to Tibet.

The latter arrive with a consciousness shaped by emotive language that leads them to see themselves on a mission. It is a civilizing mission evoking the language of superiority and inferiority, and in this regard the underlying thought collective resembles that of our other examples. Such language leads to a scenario familiar to our other cases, a conviction that the inferior are historically destined to give way to the superior.

HISTORICAL BACKGROUND

Tibet lies outside of the territory traditionally considered by the West as part of China. And it is historically true that Tibet was an independent land for many centuries, with its own ruling elite and indigenous Buddhist form of religion. That elite would periodically recognize the power and authority of the Chinese emperor (often a fellow Buddhist), but doing so did not result in any day-to-day interference by Chinese authorities. It was hoped, however, that it did mean the Chinese would offer assistance in resisting invasion from the West (such as British India) and expansionist European colonial forces. These forces (and their allied Christian missionaries) were seen by the Tibetans as *tendra* or "enemies of the Dharma" (Buddhist religion) (Laird 2006, 222). To facilitate this relationship, the Chinese kept a "residential commissioner," or Amban, with a bodyguard of 1,500 soldiers, in Tibet's capital city of Lhasa. The commissioner usually had few administrative staff, spoke no Tibetan, and rarely went out of the city. In any practical sense, the Amban could be no more than a liaison between the Chinese imperial government and official Tibetan rulers such as the Dalai Lama. In other words, the Amban functioned as an ambassador. It was an arrangement similar to what occasionally existed between China and the lands of Vietnam, Korea, and Thailand, and it is easy to see why the Tibetans never considered this arrangement a formal relinquishment of their independence.

In 1793, the Qianlong imperial government of China attempted to change this arrangement. It put forth a document entitled "Twenty-nine Articles on the Reconstruction of Tibetan Domestic Affairs," which asserted the residential commissioner's authority over much of Tibet's domestic and foreign affairs, including taxation, military and religious appointments, and the criminal courts. Although this document certainly reflected the picture of the relationship that lay in the heads of the Chinese authorities, it was a gesture that did not go much beyond theory. Tibet was a remote and vast territory, and moving beyond intent in any practical way was as yet impossible. Even one hundred years later, the Tibetans considered the Amban as a "tea-brewing commissioner," which meant that the representative of the Chinese court did little else than distribute alms to Buddhist monasteries (Wang and Shakya 2009, 39). So the situation throughout the Qing dynasty (1726 to 1911) was one of make-believe Chinese sovereignty over Tibet.

The British, seeking expanded trade out of India, actually did invade and temporarily occupy Tibet in 1904. The Chinese protested but did not defend the Tibetans, and the famous British diplomat Lord Curzon called the connection between the two lands a "constitutional fiction" (Wang and Shakya 2009, 100). Nonetheless, after the British left Tibet, the Chinese reasserted their claim of sovereignty, and the residential commissioners once more symbolically represented this claim. They were encouraged to do so by what was now a well-founded fear of Western invasion through Tibet. Simultaneously, the Tibetans, while respectful and posing no threat to the returning Chinese ambassadors, went ahead and did as they pleased.

When the Qing dynasty fell in 1911, Tibet's de facto independence was complete. The years that followed found China in a continually weaker state, and at the continuing mercy of outside invaders. After 1912 there was no residential commissioner in Tibetan capital of Lhasa, and the thirteenth Dalai Lama, Thupten Gyatso (1876–1933), who was known as a very tough and willful person, was soon the country's sole leader (Laird 2006, 213). This Dalai Lama began modernizing Tibet with the introduction of banks and a postal service, as well as reorganizing the Tibetan army on the British model; he believed these reforms were necessary to the continued independence of the country. But reform brought destabilizing tensions to Tibet. If you modernize, the implication is that what came before is no longer satisfactory. Soon there was a debate about what had held the nation back, and religion, along with the Dalai Lama's political power, became a target of the Tibetan modernists. At that point, in the 1920s, the Dalai Lama slowed the reform process. In particular, he purged the Tibetan army of those officers who disapproved of the central role of religion in the nation's political affairs.

Tibet's independence would last until 1950. The Chinese had not forgotten about Tibet and had never relinquished their claim to sovereignty over that territory, however tenuous. Those claims were strongly reasserted after the Communists took control of the Chinese government. The People's Republic was founded in 1949, and the very next year 40,000 soldiers of the Peoples Liberation Army (PLA) invaded Tibet to "liberate" the country from "imperialist forces" (Laird 2006, 318). From that point on, Tibet was truly controlled by China, whose claim to sovereignty was confirmed by military occupation.

Because the Chinese Communist Party (CCP) was still consolidating its hold over China proper and, in addition, the Korean War was now raging, Tibet was not rapidly transformed despite Chinese military occupation. Local affairs stayed much as they were before the invasion, albeit with many more Chinese officials and soldiers present. The Chinese called their agreement with Tibet the "one country, two systems" arrangement. The one country was China, who as yet tolerated the traditional "system" of Tibet. This situation was formalized under a "Seventeen-Point Agreement" announced in May of 1951.

While the "feudal serf system," as the Chinese characterized the rural situation of Tibet, and the Dalai Lama's position as head of the Tibetan government were left intact as far as Beijing was concerned, the situation inevitably became muddled. The fourteenth (and present) Dalai Lama, who was but a teenager when all this was happening, was already attempting to reform the feudal system, but met resistance from traditionalists who saw the peasants as their source of wealth. Now this was complicated by Chinese demands that the peasants supply food and other material to support their occupying army. Hardly beyond boyhood, the Dalai Lama, as the ruler of the nation, was now caught between the demands of the CCP and the Tibetan elites. In the end, the Dalai Lama decided to cooperate as best he could with the Chinese. They were overwhelmingly powerful and, although there was sporadic resistance, open rebellion would mean more bloodshed than he was willing to risk (Laird 2006, 316–317, 320).

Under the Seventeen-Point Agreement, the Dalai Lama accepted Tibet's status as part of China and acceded to Beijing's control of Tibet's foreign affairs. China, in turn, granted Tibet autonomy (the area of the Tibetan plateau was soon named the Tibetan Autonomous Region or TAR) and made no move to challenge its social and economic systems, which were often tribal based, or its Buddhist religious system. Politically, the CCP set up various committees that corresponded to the governing hierarchy in China proper. At this stage, however, they were filled mostly with people drawn from the local Tibetan ruling families. As Wang Lixiong, a Chinese writer and human rights activist with an intimate knowledge of modern Tibet, has noted, this arrangement amounted to a rather odd "alliance between [China's] communists and the Tibetan ruling class" (Wang and Shakya 2009, 43). This lasted through much of the 1950s.

The arrangement did not apply to adjacent territory, however, such as Sichuan, Yunnan, Gansu, and Qinghai, where the majority population was Han Chinese but where also were found a very large Tibetan minority. In addition, the Chinese annexed the Tibetan territories of Kham and Amdo into these adjacent areas. Almost half of the Tibetan population ended up outside of the Autonomous Region. In these territories, the same transformations going on in the rest of China (nationwide collectivization in 1955, the setting up of cadres to carry on "class struggle" against local elites in 1956) were instituted. There was significant resistance to these moves among the local Tibetans, and by the time the PLA had put down a series of rebellions, some 60,000 Tibetans had fled into the TAR. As part of the suppression of this resistance, there was substantial destruction of Buddhist religious sites throughout these regions. The upheaval caused increased fear within autonomous Tibet, for even though the CCP had promised a delay of six years (counting from 1956) for any similar "reforms," the writing was on the wall.

The sensitivity level of the elite in the TAR now went way up. For instance, when free secular schools were introduced into the TAR, they were immediately interpreted as a threat to monastery-based education. When the Chinese government paid wages to Tibetan laborers working on road construction in autonomous Tibet, it was interpreted as an attack on the traditional unpaid labor service due the rural elites. Recruiting individual TAR Tibetans with serf or peasant backgrounds into the Communist Party was seen as a violation of the traditional Tibetan social hierarchy. To a certain extent, Chinese policies toward the TAR had made things worse for the

Party's efforts in the region. On the one hand, the leaders in Beijing had decided to cooperate with the Tibetan elites in order to win official sovereignty over Tibet while avoiding major resistance; yet the problems of 1955 and 1956 had alienated much of the elite from this alliance. On the other hand, whatever they did do in that area to improve the lives of the poor majority was marked by hesitancy (so as not to alienate the elite), and this meant that they were not really winning the hearts and minds of the poor, most of whom remained wedded to traditional ways. As a consequence everyone, poor and well-to-do alike, continued to see the Chinese as colonial intruders. They were implementing a no-win policy.

TIBETAN BUDDHISM AND THE QUESTION OF CULTURAL SURVIVAL

In 1959 there was a major rebellion in the TAR against Chinese rule. Chinese troops entered the autonomous region, and the Dalai Lama fled to India, where he established a government in exile. He was soon followed by an initial 30,000 refugees. The Tibetan lower classes supported the 1959 rebellion despite being the possible beneficiaries of future Chinese reforms. In their localness they did not exist in such a future. They still existed in the present of Tibetan tradition.

The lesson that the Chinese authorities took from the troubles of 1959 was that the Seventeen-Point Agreement was a failure. And so, after the deaths of perhaps 86,000 Tibetans, and once Lhasa (where most of the rebellion was centered) was secured, the CCP adopted a new approach much more in tune with what was happening in the rest of China. Here is how Wang Lixiong describes what happened: "Work teams composed of tens of thousands of military personnel and civilian cadres were sent to every village and rural area to launch 'democratic reforms' and to determine 'class status' among the

Tibetans as a whole. The first step was to get the Tibetan masses to 'vent their grievances' and 'find the roots of their misery' asking questions such as 'Who is feeding whom?'" (Wang and Shakya 2009, 52). What this translated into was a concerted and long-term effort to change the pictures in the heads of the lower classes of the TAR so that they conformed with those of official Chinese perceptions.

Within a relatively short time, the Chinese effort had created a loyal, if limited, following for the CCP among the Tibetan poor. There were to be real benefits for making this alliance, and it came through land reform. Ninety-seven percent of the monasteries in the TAR were shut down and their extensive land holdings redistributed to those who once had the status of serfs. This at once struck a blow at religion in its institutional form and provided resources to recruit the cooperation of the masses. All those deemed upper class and participants in the recent rebellion also lost their property, which was redistributed to the landless poor. Simultaneously, the Tibetan masses were freed from the obligatory tithes they traditionally paid to the now defunct monasteries.

Nonetheless, it was an uphill battle for the Chinese cadres. Tibetan society did not have a history of class tensions, much less violence. The religious outlook that underlay Tibetan culture taught that one should spiritually rise above the travails of the present in order to create and maintain the necessary karma for rebirth into a better life. This meant that Tibetan culture had a strong element of religiously inspired passivity in it. If Tibet was to be culturally transformed, religion would have to be weakened among the masses. The long-term goal was, no doubt, to transfer this religious dedication to the revolutionary agenda of the CCP.

Wang Lixiong has a theory along this line. For ages the Tibetan people had been acculturated to the view that salvation lay in the "blissful hereafter." The key to that hereafter lay in the teachings of the Buddhist monks, to whom the masses were seemingly devoted. "It was impossible," Lixiong asserts, "to overthrow centuries of worship without playing the role of a new god who came trampling on the old one, proclaiming the dawn of a new era and instituting a new system of punishment and rewards." And that is what Mao Zedong and the CCP would attempt to do. Mao was meant to replace the Dalai Lama "as the god in their minds" (Wang and Shakya 2009, 59).

Not all experts on modern Tibet buy this theory. Tsering Shakya, a Tibetan historian and teacher, takes issue with the implication that the Tibetan masses fell for this revolutionary bait-and-switch game and thereby became "active participants in the destruction of their own culture." Rather, he asserts, those who did cooperate with the Chinese in the late 1950s and 1960s were compelled to do so by CCP pressure (they were "people with bayonets at their backs"), and so the individual had the choice of cooperation with the Party's program or punishment. On the other hand, Shakya does concede that, as in the rest of China, some Tibetans did raise Mao "to the level of a god," displacing the Buddha with the "brilliant rays of the Chairman." And at least some of the Tibetan peasantry did succumb to "a frenzied fervor, generated by the Party and ritually reinforced by its propaganda machine" (Wang and Shakya 2009, 83–84, 93–97).

Whatever explanation one favors, the CCP cadres in Tibet did work hard from 1960 to 1966 and did manage to create a limited communist base among the masses. There were beginnings of a transference of the psyche of a people from one perceptual paradigm to another. Then in 1966, when the Cultural Revolution broke over China, including Tibet, there was enough enthusiastic support in Tibet to make it look like the popular upheaval of 1959 but with the targets reversed.

What came next, the outbreak of the Cultural Revolution in Tibet, is something that moderate and traditional Tibetans have difficulty even discussing. It saw the "active participation" of the Tibetan peasantry "in leveling the very temples and monasteries they had once held most sacred" (Wang and Shakya 2009, 61). On the other hand, hundreds of thousands of Tibetans were imprisoned, and some 173,000 died in the prisons and work camps of that era. These were the ones who refused to be, in Thomas Laird's words, "terrorized into assimilation" (Laird 2006, 348). Nonetheless, a significant number of Tibetans participated in the destruction of the symbols of their own culture. Of these years the tenth Panchen Lama, the second highest-ranking Lama after the Dalai Lama, wrote: "Once a nationality's language, costume, customs, and other important characteristics have disappeared, then the nationality itself has disappeared— that is say, it has turned into another nationality" (Laird 2006, 348). That was certainly the intent of the Cultural Revolution in Tibet—to move the country in the direction of cultural genocide, or perhaps more accurately in this case, cultural suicide.

The Cultural Revolution was a classic case study for the destructive power of a thought collective. You take a population, in this case the core of Han Chinese youth along with recruits from the ethnic minorities, and raise them over the course of a generation to a particular ideology and perceptual paradigm. And at a certain point you can find a significant percentage of that population (though not all) more than ready to act aggressively in line with a particular message. Indeed, they may initiate action for the sake of ideological purity or in defense of their worldview, without any signal from authority. Authority might be dragged along after the fact. In the case of China's Cultural Revolution, it was a combination of spontaneous action on the part of the indoctrinated and encouragement from the top.

In 1969, the Chinese government introduced a system of people's communes into Tibet. In other words, the redistributed land that had been a large part of the material benefit the Tibetan peasant had derived from the destruction of the monasteries and accompanying "class struggle" was now taken from them through a process of collectivization. The result was an armed revolt in Tibet in that same year. It was an economically driven affair, and a reversal of the cultural destruction wrought by the events of 1966 was not one of its aims. This revolt, of course, failed.

The processes of Cultural Revolution in Tibet went on until the end of the 1970s. Mao died in 1976, and Deng Xiaoping became China's supreme leader in 1978. By 1980 the Cultural Revolution had been suppressed, and the people's communes program in Tibet ended. The new strategy was built on the assumption that the key to stability was "development." As Wang Lixiong explains, Beijing believed that "so long as the economy keeps developing and the living standard keeps improving, people will feel settled and happy. In the meantime, conflicts over nationality will gradually die off" (Wang and Shakya 2009, 157). This was a variant on the "full belly theory of imperialism," and there can be little doubt that things did in fact materially improve in the TAR during Deng's time.

Nonetheless, this was not a smooth or easy transition away from the ideological radicalism of the Cultural Revolution. For fourteen years, Han Chinese cadres had been at work in Tibet following the dictates of revolutionary ideology, and they had drawn into their orbit a significant number of Tibetan nationals whose careers were made along these same lines. Now they were told by Beijing that it was all "a mistake." Resistance to change on the part of these cadres was strong. Also strong was the conviction by many ordinary Tibetans that they were in the hands of an unpredictable and fickle regime. As for the Tibetan peasants, their attitude was described (about 1980) by one village headman as follows: "No one wants to work for the old nobles for free again, but everyone wants the Chinese to leave and the Dalai Lama to return. . . . The new nobles are all Chinese and they are even harsher than the old ones" (Laird 2006, 340). Thus, despite the movement away from ideological radicalism, there were renewed disturbances in 1987 that reflected the unease of traditionalists with confusing societal changes and ongoing tensions between the CCP and the monastic movement, which was trying to reassert itself. The troubles coincided with the Dalai Lama's appearance before a committee of the U.S. Congress in 1987. The result was a brief imposition of martial law in 1989. After that things remained relatively stable in Tibet.

A new set of guidelines had been announced for TAR that are, more or less, still in effect today. They include: 1) Tibet should have autonomous status; 2) economic policies for the TAR should be attuned to local circumstances and practical goals rather than being ideologically structured (a measure that resulted in rising living standards throughout the TAR); 3) Han Chinese cadres should be replaced by ethnic Tibetan cadres (though the economically moti-vated inflow of ethnic Chinese into Tibet continues apace); and 4) Tibetan culture should be strengthened.

Item 4 mainly focused on the goal of using of the Tibetan lan-guage in all official documents and speeches, in the schools and places of employment. This would prove difficult to accomplish, since most of the educated Tibetans who were considered trustwor-thy by the CCP now spoke Mandarin Chinese, rather than Tibetan. Despite the intent of the declaration, urban-based education con-tinued to be carried on in Mandarin (which, for economic reasons, many Tibetan city dwellers preferred for their children), as were all courses at the university level except those on Tibetan literature. However, Tibetan was now used in the rural schools. This tended to divide the country culturally. Soon it was mostly children from rural Tibet who went to the monasteries for education, while the urban elites become at least superficially acculturated into the Chinese lifestyle. Thus, despite the CCP's lip service to preserving the Tibetan language, it has in fact been marginalized.

"Strengthening Tibetan culture" also called for "respect for the people's normal religious practices" (Wang and Shakya 2009, 70). This was very important. According to the Panchen Lama, writing in 1962, Tibetan Buddhism was on the verge of being "virtually annihilated" (Shakya 1999, 271). If this fate, essentially amounting to cultural genocide, was to be avoided, cultivation of the Tibetan Buddhist religion was essential.

A Strategy of Cultural Genocide?

The inclusion of "normal religious practices," a seminal aspect of Tibetan culture, should have slowed any cultural erosion or transformation. And, indeed, the number of Buddhist monks and nuns in Tibet increased to about 46,000 by 1994 (Wang and Shakya 2009, 72). Some of the old temples and monasteries were rebuilt (and often turned into tourist sites) or new ones constructed. However, as it turned out, the cultural question was far from settled.

A key factor here was that those who were to be in charge of overseeing the "strengthening of Tibetan culture" were perforce Tibetan nationals who were confirmed CCP loyalists. Since the 1950s, the Chinese have built up an alternative educational system to the monastic education traditional to Tibet. What this has produced is a split within generations as well as one between generations. Those educated in the Chinese-sponsored schools or in China itself were considered more "modern" than those educated in the monasteries, who retained a traditional outlook. It was the former who were always chosen for important positions in the TAR. So, although Tibetans were now in all the key positions, and in the majority on all the representative bodies in the TAR, they were there because they would reflect Party goals for local culture, among other things, and not traditional sentiments.

This included overseeing "the people's normal religious practices." The Tibetan communists knew that the monks and nuns had been in the lead of national resistance, and their job was to not allow this to continue under the new "liberal" (post-Cultural Revolution) conditions. In other words, their job was to manage Tibetan religious and cultural self-expression. Superficially, this would not be hard to accomplish: almost the entire religious leadership of Tibet was in exile by the late 1980s, and no new leadership figures, such as the Panchen Lama, could be appointed within Tibet without CCP approval.

Thus, while some monasteries were rebuilt and traditional arts cultivated, no reference to Tibetan nationalism, to the Dalai Lama, or to Tibetan Buddhism's traditional connection to political thought, governance, or national self-identity was allowed. This, of course, was an explicit admission on the part of Beijing that Tibetan Buddhism, the essence of Tibetan culture, was essentially tied to Tibetan nationalism. In the eyes of the Party leadership this tended to accentuate fears that real cultural autonomy would inevitably lead to demands for independence. By the end of the 1980s police surveillance was high in Tibet, and censors watched for "mistakes" reflecting too much cultural independence, particularly of the religious kind, and punished those who made them.

The fate of the female Tibetan writer Woeser, as described by Wang and Shakya in the book *The Struggle for Tibet*, is a good example of this situation. Woeser was the editor of *Tibetan Literature*, the official journal of the Tibetan Literature Association in the

TAR. In 2003, she edited and contributed to a prose anthology (written in Chinese) entitled *Notes on Tibet*, which sold well throughout Tibet and China. Somehow the book attracted the attention of the censors only after publication, and Woeser was belatedly accused of "serious political mistakes." The TAR Literature Association, of which Woeser was a member, was ordered to "examine" the book for political appropriateness. Here is some of what it concluded: 1) the work "exaggerates and beautifies the positive function of religion in social life"; 2) the work makes false value judgments and divorces itself from correct political principles; and 3) the work "praises the fourteenth Dalai Lama . . . and encourages reverence to, and belief in, religion."

As if the case sought to emulate in reverse that of Galileo, Woeser (who defended religion) was required to submit to a period of "self-criticism" entailing repeated interrogations that would lead to a forced confession. In order to escape this ordeal, Woeser went into exile in late 2003. As in the case of Galileo, Woeser's treatment served as a warning to other native residents of Tibet to accept CCP guidance. Or, as Wang Lixiong puts it, "The system that feeds the cultural is also the system that disciplines it totally. Fear of the system precludes resistance against it." He goes on to explain, "Dissidents are not tolerated by the system which dominates Tibet's cultural space almost completely, and a cultural market that is at least partially independent of the official system has yet to emerge in the Tibetan province" (Wang and Shakya 2009, 123, 144). The resulting "silence" is then taken by the authorities as evidence of acquiescence and stability in Tibet. Thus the CCP is in the process of remaking Tibetan culture in its own image. Tibetan culture means what the Party says it means. In the process, the indigenous Tibetans are slowly but surely going through a transformation that is equivalent to cultural genocide.

We may also carry this picture into China itself. The Chinese people now think of Tibet as part of China proper. They believe that whereas Tibet was a primitive and barbaric place before its integration into China, now it is a modernizing province with religious freedom that sustains a spiritual Buddhist legacy worthy of admiration (Wang and Shakya 2009, 259, 266). This picture is the one that is painted by Chinese media and government spokespeople. The Chinese public has no way of independently testing these claims, any more than did the urban-based colonials in reference to Indians on the American frontier. The picture painted in their heads may indeed be a distorted one, but their localism guarantees that, under normal conditions, propaganda stands in for reality.

Back in Tibet, the Chinese policy of directly controlling Tibetan Buddhism has actually undercut the spiritual uniqueness many Chinese attribute to it. It has done this by corrupting the religious leadership residing in Tibet. The leadership is traditionally associated with the monasteries, and the monasteries have traditionally been the mediator between the Buddhist philosophy of self-discipline and the devaluation of the material world, on the one hand, and the superstitions and worldly orientation of popular belief on the other. If the leadership is adulterated, the monasteries will tend to lose their ability to instruct the common believers in moral self-discipline.

A precedent for something of this sort was set immediately after the 1959 uprising in Tibet. At that time, formal practice of Tibetan Buddhism was interrupted. Religious institutions, including almost all of the 600-plus Buddhist educational centers were closed, and monks and nuns were forced to take up ordinary lives. This went on through the Cultural Revolution. By the time this era ended, in the 1980s, not only was the hierarchal structure of the religion in disarray (many traditional religious leaders had gone into exile) but a generation of Tibetans had now grown up under the anti-religious teachings of the CCP. So, although there was a religious recovery in Tibet after the death of Mao, it was never a full one. Even under the relaxed post–Cultural Revolution environment, any move to recreate the monastic orders on a large scale has been stopped. No official intercommunication between monasteries is allowed. As of 2003, there were ninety-three Buddhist educational centers in Tibet, eighty-four of which were unregistered with the government and thus illegal (Wang and Shakya 2009, 173). Essentially, in the post–Cultural Revolution era, the CCP has continued to erode the theological and philosophical basis of Tibetan Buddhism. If they succeed, all that will be left to the religion is superstition and formulaic practices. It is those remnants which the CCP hope will die away as material improvements proceed.

In 1998, during a visit of President Bill Clinton to China, Communist Party Secretary Jiang Zemin made clear the stunted role left to religion, both in Tibet and the rest of China. He said, "We won't allow religion to be used to confront the leadership of the Party and the socialist system" (Wang and Shakya 2009, 176). The Tibetan religious hierarchy will not be allowed to compete with the CCP hierarchy for the loyalty of Tibetans. As a consequence, all Buddhist officials and leaders within Tibet are now chosen or approved by communist officials. These are people who have been required to study in government-sanctioned Buddhist academies. Following this strategy, there is no need to suppress the Buddhist religion entirely, as Mao and the Cultural Revolution's Red Guards sought to do. One simply destroys it as an independent system with an autonomous leadership, thereby transforming it into an innocuous shadow of its former self. One remakes it into something safe and compatible with the CCP worldview.

The program of remaking the Tibetan thought collective has already gone a long way. For instance, according to Tsering Shakya, there is an increasing cultural gap between the indigenous Tibetans who have been experiencing the influence of China for repeated generations and those who now reside in exile. When those who have grown up in one community meet those who have grown up in the other, they often have trouble communicating. Shakya tells us that the exiles "see themselves as the 'true' representatives of Tibetanness, and the Tibetans inside [China] as merely passive, oppressed victims." Sometimes this has resulted in real personal tragedy. When in 1995 Dadon, Tibet's most popular singer, went into exile in India, she found that she was practically unknown in the exile community, and her popular contemporary songs were dismissed by that audience as "Chinese-style songs." Alienated by the Chinese regime in her country, she had come to India only to find that she was even more alienated from the Tibetan exile community (Wang and Shakya 2009, 215).

Bringing the Story Up to Date

As great as the efforts toward assimilation into China have been, they are far from complete. Indeed, this sort of acculturation process must take many generations. The Tibetans are not the only ethnic minority undergoing this transformation. To date, China's multiple indigenous peoples have managed to continue to exert some level of centrifugal force to counter the central gravitational pull of Han culture and CCP ideology. In the opinion of Tsering Shakya, this is a consequence of China's attempt to "create a nation out of an empire" (Wang and Shakya 2009, 267). For that reason, Communist China has some "twenty-four provincial or ministerial-level institutions [within its] bureaucratic system that perform 'anti-separatist' roles, which represents a huge group with a considerable amount of power, personnel and resources" (Wang and

Shakya 2009, 224). In times past, and particularly under the leadership of Mao and then Deng, this many-faceted bureaucracy was
kept in check by strong centralized decision making. However, after
Deng's time decision making tended to devolve to the bureaucratic
levels themselves.

This was the bureaucratic state of things in March 2008, when
trouble broke out once more in the TAR and neighboring provinces
with significant Tibetan populations. On March 10, there were
peaceful demonstrations by monks and nuns in the capital of Lhasa
commemorating the anniversary of the 1959 Tibetan uprising. They
also put forth a demand for the release of all monks and nuns still
held in prison by the authorities. While these demonstrations were
initially nonviolent, the government's response was not, and so
things rapidly escalated and spread beyond the capital. Tensions
between ethnic Tibetans and the rapidly increasing number of Han
Chinese in the Tibetan urban centers soon turned violent. It seems
accurate to assume that events flowed, at least in part, from the
long-standing problems of social and economic discrimination
claimed by indigenous Tibetans. This was paralleled by complaints
about inflation and high unemployment among urban-based
Tibetan youth. Under these circumstances, Tibetans would find it
hard to follow Zhou Enlai's advice, given to them in the 1950s, to
"emulate the Manchus and assimilate with the Chinese" (Shakya
1999, 367). That does not mean that an increasing number of them
do not want to do so. Given the number of generations that have
grown up under the Chinese system, it may be a mistake to assume
that "separatism" or Tibetan nationalism is what these protests are
necessarily about. It could be that they are demands for equity
within the system itself. Or, as Tsering Shakya puts it, "The resistance is about the right to have a voice in the process" (Wang and
Shakya 2009, 26).

The Chinese bureaucracy does not appear to be willing, or perhaps even able, to provide that equity. The two populations have not, to date at least, intermingled so as to prevent ethnic competition and hatred. In other words, the natural localness of the two populations has remained separate. In addition, most Han Chinese are of the opinion (formed within a closed information environment) that Tibetans are materially doing better and better. Ma Lihua, a Chinese scholar very familiar with Tibet, claims that improvements in the living standards of Tibetans are not just CCP propaganda but quite real (Laird 2006, 350). So, in the eyes of many Chinese, Tibetan violence must be about something other than economics. It must be recalcitrant separatism, a form of ungratefulness or biting the hand that feeds you. The official default explanation taken up by the CCP bureaucracy in Beijing, and repeatedly broadcast throughout China proper and even on overseas Chinese-language media, has been that the events of 2008 were planned by the exiles led by the Dalai Lama and carried out by their "separatist" allies within Tibet. This storyline both guides and reflects public opinion in China and among overseas Chinese, as well, even though the Chinese authorities seem unable to produce direct supporting evidence. Just to spice the pot, so to speak, Beijing has also asserted that the violence was meant to embarrass China at a time when it was about to host the summer Olympics.

In reaction to all this, local decision makers in the antiseparatist bureaucracies acted in a formulaic way. The 2008 demonstrations were roughly put down by Han Chinese soldiers brought in for this purpose. They acted so largely because they brought with them the a priori belief that it was separatism that they were fighting. Once things were stable, a new cultural offensive was put into motion. Customs (like horse racing), local holidays, even traditional dress, were now sporadically suppressed. All Buddhist monks and nuns residing in the TAR were considered as potential agents and spies of the Dalai Lama.

According to Wang Lixiong, this heavy-handed reaction by the antiseparatist bureaucracies has actually "bred a separatist consciousness among the Tibetans" (Wang and Shakya 2009, 236–237). Thus, while the March 2008 demonstrations actually started out as socioeconomic protests, they were treated as separatist ones by bureaucrats whose thinking was shaped to a stereotyped picture of the Tibetan situation. They therefore produced a self-fulfilling prophesy, and the knee-jerk response forced at least some of the protesters to consider the possibility that there could be no resolution within the CCP system for what they perceived as racially based discrimination. They began to reconsider the goal of independence, where initially that had not been on their agenda. This is what happens when people (in this case the Chinese) cannot break out of the straitjacket of their own closed information environments.

It would appear that Tibetan Buddhism, within Chinese-controlled Tibet, is mutating into a weapon of the CCP. Thomas Laird describes this trend as an effort to "exterminate the philosophy [of Buddhism] in Tibet" (Laird 2006, 344), and that is no doubt the long-term goal. But for now what appears to be happening is the reduction of the religion to a superficial minimum so that it might better serve as a transitional medium en route to a more thoroughgoing communist-atheist future. This is what CCP guidelines, formulated in 1983, described as the "natural withering of religion" (Shakya 1999, 419). What is left of the religion that constituted the core of Tibetan culture is destined to be used to pave the way for the death of that culture.

Conclusion

Though the CCP would never use the words or describe the situation in this way, it seems clear that the ultimate goal of their policies in Tibet is the genocidal elimination of traditional Tibetan culture. How else can Tibetans be ultimately led to assimilate with the Chinese? With sufficient control over the informational environment and enough time to work the process, something approximating this radical acculturation might be possible. But the Chinese are a product of their own natural localness, which has produced a kind of "one size fits all" ideology. Their perceptions of Tibet are laced with suspicion of conspiracies cooked up by foreign and exiled foes, and their policies there are overreliant on punishment. Thus, they are always getting in their own way by producing resentment that keeps alive the very sense of "otherness" that they want the Tibetans to abandon.

In the other examples we have taken up, the perpetrators of cultural genocide always had alternative ends to fall back on. All of them were ultimately prepared to contemplate either physical genocide, mass expulsion, or severe ghettoization. The Chinese seem not to have considered these options for Tibet. Assimilation is their goal, and cultural genocide is pursued only because it is seen as a necessary step in that direction.

Finally, the core institution of traditional Tibetan culture, that is, genuine Tibetan Buddhism, with its transmission of knowledge of the Dharma over generations, has now been relocated to India and Nepal. Here monasteries and nunneries have been constructed and new monks and nuns, many born in exile, carry on the faith. In addition, an increasing number of non-Tibetans are being instructed. Ironically, what for centuries had been but a sub-branch of Buddhism practiced in the most isolated of countries has now attained worldwide status—largely thanks to the culturally destructive practices of the Chinese Communist Party.

6

CONCLUSION

The theoretical framework that has been proposed to help us understand the phenomenon of cultural genocide consists of the following major concepts: natural localism (here considered at the group level), closed information environments, and thought collectives. Let us review how each of these concepts played into the examples given in the previous chapters, making possible popular and official support for cultural genocide.

Natural Localism

In each case taken up in this book there is duality. That is, there exist two settings of localism that breed cultural paradigms: one a powerful and aggressive culture and the other a relatively weaker one. In the case of the cultural genocide committed against the North American Indians, there were two groups of people bred to a range of localisms, and there was nothing in either cultural array, be it European or American, that was anything like that of the other. When, beginning in the sixteenth century, a serious level of contact began the cultural differences were so great that they appeared, at least to the majority of the respective populations, as mutually exclusive.

Given the low population density in the Americas, it might have been possible to avoid a fatal clash of these idiosyncratic societies if it had not been for the enormous rate of immigration from Europe. Within a relatively brief time, in what essentially entailed a mass migration, the locales that were European were transferred, in their general psychological manifestations, to the shores of eastern North America. It is certainly true that the transfer to such an alien territory modified the cultures of the immigrants over time, but the resulting new amalgam was still a world apart from that of the indigenous Indians.

One can see this immediately in terms of the notion of property rights. Private property as understood in Europe had not evolved as a product of North American Indian natural localism. This was particularly true in reference to the ownership of land. On the other hand, the European settlers brought with them a notion of landed property that in many ways underpinned their geographic under-standing of the world, and they would ultimately force that notion on the Indians. As Sidner Larson has put it, "Behind the English invasion of North America, behind their massacre of Native Americans, their deception, and their brutality, was a special, powerful drive based on private property" (Larson 1997, 570).

One consequence of natural localism that the Europeans and Native Americans did share was a sense that their outlook and ways of doing things were "natural." This made it nearly impossible for the vast majority in either group to imagine the adoption of the other's way of life. The Europeans in particular infused this feeling of naturalness with an imagined divine sanction, giving them in turn, a definite sense of superiority. This feeling of superiority did have a certain basis in fact, but that rested not in any divine blessing but rather the possession of weaponry vastly superior to that of their native opponents. It was all wrapped up in a progressive civilizational package, as far as the Europeans were concerned. And that was the case regardless of which variation of the transplanted European localness we look at. It did not matter if they were Puritans in Massachusetts, Catholics in Maryland, or Scotch Presbyterians in Georgia, their attitude toward the "other" that was the American Indian was quite similar.

This ubiquitous cultural myopia led, to use a concept proposed by Arjun Appadurai, to a "predatory identity" (Appadurai 2006, 51, 83). The Indian culture was seen by the majority of European settlers as not only "abnormal" but also dangerous. For most of them there were no "noble savages." This was just a product of far-away European romantic thinkers like Rousseau. For those on the frontier, there were only threatening savages. And if they could not be sanitized by Christian missionaries, they deserved to be either isolated on reservations or wiped out altogether. Localism, in its form of a European predatory identity, would allow for no pluralism. And the power differential in the form of superior weapons sealed the outcome of this "clash of cultures."

When we move forward in time, and geographically back to Europe, to consider the duality of the czarist, Eastern Orthodox, localized environment versus that of the Jews caught within the Russian Empire, we find a similar attitudinal pattern played out against different cultural settings. Here, too, one group is vastly more powerful than the other. Once more the resulting sense of superiority is based on weaponry and confirmed by religion. Once more there is pervasive fear (though not in this case a physical one) of the threatening "other."

The scenario in the case of czarist Russia was more deeply rooted in time than the one that played itself out on the American frontier. That is, the mythology of anti-Semitism had been percolating for ages and not just a century or so. Across those ages there had been repeated episodes of attacks on Jews which, if not outright attempts at physical genocide, showed that the potential, the growing predatory identity on the part of Europe's gentiles, was there. The right circumstances for such an attempt would have to await the twentieth century. For the nineteenth-century czars, at least, the contradiction between their desire to be one with European modernity and the wholesale slaughter of the Jews under their control was too obvious.

However, that contradiction did not prevent them from attempting cultural genocide. The repeated efforts of the czars to use geographic isolation, military conscription, educational manipulation, and even forced conversion to wipe out the Jewishness of the Jews (that is, to destroy the natural localism of the Jewish communities in their midst) were all accepted and occasionally applauded by the many myth-bound Russians whose outlook was a product of an environment as isolated and distorted as that of the shtetl Jews themselves. On the other hand, the power of natural localness to set parameters on the worldview of individuals and communities at large is attested to not only by the ancient nature of anti-Semitism but also by the ability of Europe's Jews to withstand the siege generation after generation.

The subsequent adoption of a similar predatory identity by the Jewish survivors of anti-Semitism is testimony to the fact that the isolation forced upon them by gentile society had negative consequences for their resulting, inbred worldview. Suffering does not produce wisdom or build character. It produces resentment and builds up a desire for revenge that might well be displaced onto a group other than the one immediately responsible for your plight. In the prison of your localness you do not necessarily produce a refined and rational characterization of the "other." That other group can become defined in a diffuse and generalized way (as all

Indians, all white men, all Jews, all gentiles), and on that basis be assigned to any number of otherwise innocent people.

So it was with that element of the European Jews who created Israel. These Jews were not only the victims but also the products of the extreme localness enforced on them by their persecutors. The resulting outlook reflected as extreme a predatory identity as the one possessed by their anti-Semitic enemies. They were to prove this in their characterization and treatment of the Palestinians.

When the Ashkenazim (the European Jews) who participated in the Zionist movement following the 1917 Balfour Declaration immigrated to Palestine, they did not shed their European outlook. Nor, despite their general secularism, did they shed their Bible-based myths. So, on the one hand, they came to this non-Western place with the historically built-in cultural attitude of European settlers within a colonial setting. It will be remembered that, from 1917 through 1948, Palestine was a League of Nations (and then a United Nations) Mandate territory given over to British rule. The Zionists had made an alliance with the British based on the Balfour Declaration, and so came into Palestine as European settlers under British protection.

On the other hand, the Jews had long incorporated reference to Jerusalem in their prayers and festivals, and this gave both the observant and nonobservant among them a sense of connection to Palestine in general and Jerusalem in particular, although very few of them had ever been there. Leaving aside the question of whether one can read the Bible as history, the connection with the Holy Land for the vast majority of Jews was, in actuality, an "imagined" one. It was the product of over one thousand years of oral story telling passed down in an environment of enforced localness.

By the time of World War II and the Nazi Holocaust, relations had thoroughly deteriorated between Jewish immigrants in Palestine and the indigenous Arab population. The latter, too, were products of a natural localness that was underpinned by a relationship with the land that was not imagined but immediately real. They and their ancestors had always been in situ. And so, to some extent, the scenario of the American frontier was played out in the Holy Land. The Zionists sometimes saw it that way and occasionally referred to themselves as latter-day pilgrims and puritans, and the Arabs as similar to "Apaches." And, in fact, the Zionists did actually resemble, in terms of their intentions, the seventeenth- and eighteenth-century migrants to North America. In both cases Europeans, born and bred by the ages of their local history, had a sense of cultural and ideological superiority that was backed up with technology that was indeed superior. They invaded a non-European place and took for themselves someone else's land. And, once again, neither the conqueror nor the conquered could share the other's perspective. Both were bound to their cultural paradigms.

Finally, natural localism set the stage for the ongoing confrontation between the Tibetans and the Chinese. Tibet always was, and to some extent still is, one of the most isolated places on the globe. In that isolation, it developed a deeply idiosyncratic culture and its own version of the Buddhist religion. The church and state had long been melded together in Tibet when, beginning in the nineteenth century, the outside world started encroaching on that land in earnest. First came the British invasion of Tibet through India, and then the Chinese occupation in the post–World War II period. That latter occupation is ongoing.

The Chinese occupation set the stage for a serious clash of cultures—of competing localisms. Beijing's ruling ideology is its own brand of communism. That made the cultural paradigm from which the Chinese conquerers worked one that was stubbornly antireligious while itself having the fervor of a religion. The Chinese varied their strategy in Tibet between a gradualist approach and wholesale attempts to impose radical communism overnight. It soon became apparent that neither tactic would really work as long as the key structural aspect of Tibetan culture—that is, Tibetan Buddhism—was left intact. On the other hand, the experiences of the Cultural Revolution in Tibet had demonstrated just how deeply rooted Buddhism was. You could destroy its temples and, over time, the locals would just rebuild them.

The Chinese have gone back to a gradualist approach that now seeks not to wipe out Buddhism in Tibet but to transform it, to redefine it, in ways congenial to Chinese rule. Given that Buddhism is integral to traditional Tibetan culture, this is in fact a strategy of cultural genocide in slow motion.

Beijing now controls the administration of the religion and dictates what its hierarchy can and cannot teach or pass down to following generations. The religious teachings that supplied the Tibetans with a sophisticated notion of their relationship with nature based on self-discipline, a set of moral principles, and a respect for Buddhist leaders of high achievement is being lost. The religion is devolving to a lowest common denominator of superstition and ritual. As this happens, the traditional Tibetan culture becomes but a shadow of its former self. It is the opinion of the leaders in Beijing that at this level, Tibetan Buddhism will not be able to compete with the development and modernity they are introducing into Tibet. Over time, they believe, the religion will wither away.

CLOSED INFORMATION ENVIRONMENTS

Natural localism lends itself to the creation of closed information environments for all but local affairs. Local happenings are, of course, open to firsthand investigation. Contextual knowledge is ready at hand, and on its basis critical judgments are possible. Information that does not match up with personal experience is not likely to be given much credence. However, events that are farther afield are not experienced at firsthand by the vast majority of local inhabitants. The range of knowledge one has is limited, and the contextual knowledge necessary for critical thinking is mostly lacking. The source of information on such events, which will almost always be stylized to conform with the popular culture, is a closed one and often limited to certain official government or establishment sources.

The men and women who came over the Atlantic Ocean in increasing numbers did not have any firsthand knowledge of North American Indians. And the same can be said for most of the people who settled down in what became the thirteen British colonies along the eastern seaboard of North America. In only the very earliest of these settlements did relatively common face-to-face interactions take place, and it was in that context that the clash of alien localisms and their apparently incompatible cultural paradigms took place. Once that clash developed, most of the Indian peoples were physically pushed away from the European settlements, and the ongoing struggle between the two competing parties would play out at some remove from the average colonial settler's local world.

A greater number of the Indian peoples were familiar with the Europeans because their entire communities were taking the brunt of European expansion. However, those further back from the zone of conflict were at least temporarily ignorant of what was coming. This means that both groups removed from the frontier would perceive and understand the struggle from point of natural localism. From that point, they could know only what they were told by individuals filtering back from the frontier, by the inevitable rumor mill built on hearsay, or (in the case of the European colonies) by what they were taught by those who held community authority, be they politicians, writers of novels, or those who passed for journalists. The knowledge of these "authorities" was almost always second-hand and often laced with emotive feelings bred of conflict. There was no one operating as the equivalent of a fact checker.

The information environment also had to conform to the given cultural paradigm. In the case of the Europeans, this paradigm emphasized civilizational superiority backed up by divine blessing. The Indians' failure to live by European standards (for instance, in the practice of private property in land) was interpreted as proof of their backwardness. Yet, even in those few cases where Indian tribes did adapt to the European standards of civilization, including Christianity (one thinks here of the Cherokee), the information provided by the closed environment, interlaced as it was with obsessive racism, resulted in a firm conviction of the ultimate incapability of peoples. So strong were these factors that they could override the fact—the very reality—of Indian adaptation and result in the eviction of the weaker party. In the case of President Andrew Jackson and his allies versus the Cherokee Indians, not even the laws of the United States could derail this culturally rationalized path of action.

The history of the American colonies and the centuries of relentless displacement of indigenous populations give us an example of the power of a closed information environment. Our perception of reality for events ongoing but at a distance is based on the information supplied to us by outside sources, and on that we base our decisions and actions. The story told by that information, despite the fact that it is not necessarily accurate or true, shapes our lives.

When we move to the example of the Russian czars and their confrontation with the Jews, we find a similar situation. For centuries the Russians, as well as other Europeans, were told that the Jews were dangerous aliens. This was conveyed in the most emotive sort of language having to do with the death of Christ, the manipulation of economies, and the desecration of cultures. As was the case on the American frontier, the average Russian citizen would have had little access to countervailing information and little or no direct inter-action with the "other." The resulting lack of adequate contextual knowledge meant that people could not make a critical judgment on the situation, even if it occurred to them that this was necessary. This is the important point. Within a closed information environ-ment, the information one gets is so consistent and ubiquitous that most people will see no need to question it. They will take it as obvious truth.

This is so not only for the average citizen. It also applies to the leaders and opinion makers, in this case the czars and their entourage, the officialdom of the Russian Orthodox Church, and the massive bureaucracy that ran the vast Russian empire in the nineteenth and early twentieth centuries. The information they passed on to the public was the stuff they, too, believed. On the face of it, these people were an educated group with a much broader horizon than the Russian peasant or town dweller. Most important, they had access to allegedly enlightened ideas of Western Europe. But they were suspicious of these ideas and feared that they would undermine Russia's traditional culture and thus the social and political status quo on which their authority and power rested. The assumptions underlying their policy decisions and their structuring of the "news" for others were consistent with the culture and historical worldview they shared with the general citizenry.

As we have seen, many of the early twentieth-century Jews who were persecuted by the Russian czars, often with the support of the general citizenry, would eventually find their way to Palestine. There they collectively created a new closed information environ-ment based on the assumption that they, just like the European colonizers of the New World, had a God-given right to settle this land and were now surrounded by enemies who, if given a chance, would destroy them and their superior culture. They would eventually explicitly identify these enemies not only with "Apaches" but also with the European anti-Semites who constituted their historical persecutors. From the time of their mass immigration into Palestine, the Jews involved shaped their information environment to this message. Because their schooling and media adopted it, and the resistance offered to their settlement by the Palestinians seemed to confirm it, the "pictures in their heads" made these assumptions appear to be bald-faced truth. To get outside of this closed information environment, the Jewish Israeli must purposely go looking for countervailing information. And indeed, it was and is there to find if he or she looks hard enough. But it is a function of natural localness that most do not look at all, much less with persistence and objectivity. If they happen upon it by accident, as it were, their learned assumptions are usually well enough embedded that they readily dismiss whatever challenges their worldview.

The same process can be seen taking place in today's China when it comes to perceptions of Tibet. The vast majority of the information available to the average Chinese citizen about what its own government is doing in far-off Tibet is supplied by government sources. To get beyond this description takes work, and since Tibet does not impinge upon the local lives of most Chinese, it rarely occurs to them to go and seek alternative story lines.

In Tibet itself there exists an actual culture war, that is, a struggle between two closed information environments, the one of traditional Tibetan culture and the other of the new Chinese Tibet. The promoters of the latter are determined to displace the former, and they have the power to do so. All they apparently need is the time and the patience to make it so.

THOUGHT COLLECTIVES

As natural localism lends itself to the creation of closed information environments, so do these lend themselves to thought collectives. It will be remembered that if a consistent stylized story line is presented to the public, across the media spectrum and over a sufficiently long time, it will produce generally similar pictures in the heads of local, regional, and even national populations. What results is a thought collective. Such community-wide perspectives take on added strength from the fact that most people shape their opinions to coincide with those around them. Once the shared perspective is in place, there is a natural tendency to reinforce it by seeking out information that supports it and ignoring or downplaying what does not. This happened in the case of each of our examined episodes.

The thought collective that developed in the American colonies was a variation on the theme of civilization expanding against the frontiers of barbarism. Here the noble savage of Rousseau and even the relatively benign Mohegans of the novels of James Fenimore Copper (benign because that tribe was friendly to the British colonists) are left behind for the bloody savage of the stereotyped frontier. Once the stylized message of the closed information environment has produced a thought collective, its perception-shaping force will become ubiquitous. Thus, the children, the elderly, and everyone in between will actively or passively hold it as true. For instance, when on December 16, 1773, American colonists who called themselves the "sons of liberty" decided to turn Boston harbor into large pond of iced tea, they choose to disguise themselves as Indians. It made no difference that there probably had not been Indians of any number in the city of Boston for a hundred years; the image of the Indian is what appeared to fit the needs of the moment. For who were the vandals of American folklore? Everyone knew that it was the Indians.

It is this stylized thought collective that allowed the dispossession and cultural destruction of the native population. When, well into this process, the Cherokees were forcibly moved westward by the U.S. Army under the (illegal) orders of President Andrew Jackson, there was very little public objection. The Cherokees had conformed to the demands that they "Americanize." However, by doing so they made themselves an anomaly—a culturally suspect exception to the stereotype of the Indian savage. Quite apart from the wanton greed for land that motivated the white citizens of Georgia, there was no place in the dominant thought collective for the general American population to slot the anomalous Cherokee. Not being able to make much sense of the Cherokee, most Americans must have either paid no attention to their plight or defaulted to the culturally compatible position that they were savages pretending to be civilized people, which in the end was really an impossible status for any Indian to achieve. In such an exceptional situation, the stereotypes of the thought collective will prevail.

The only members of the American white population who would potentially break out of the thought collective were those with first-hand contextual knowledge that contradicted the stereotyped picture of the Indians. In the case of the Cherokee, this would have been the missionaries who had worked so hard to transform the tribe. Confronted with the popular reaction from Christian America, ranging from indifference to hostility, they must have been truly confused and alienated. Those missionaries who attempted to stand by the Cherokee were threatened with arrest and violence by Georgia authorities.

The thought collective that prevailed in nineteenth-century Russia in relation to the Jews was anti-Semitism. This was an age-old phenomenon particularly virulent at this time in Russia due to the degree that the country's closed information environment was isolated from outside influences. Russian popular culture actively resisted the more progressive notions of Western Europe, and the liberation of the Jews was associated with those progressive ideas. Specifically, they were associated with Napoleonic reforms, and Napoleon had invaded Russia. He and his ideas were seen as quite alien.

We have seen that anti-Semitism's ancient roots helped it appear self-evidently true in an environment where only those influenced by the alien West tended to question it. For many, longevity must have constituted proof of its truth. It was also connected to the popular notion of the death of Christ and therefore bound to a core element of Christianity. Christianity, in turn, was yet another foundational aspect of the broader prevailing Russian thought collective. Ultimately, it would take a bloody revolution to shake the nation's attachment to anti-Semitism, and then only imperfectly. Stalin, in his paranoia, would return to the theme late in his career as Russia's absolute leader.

The power of anti-Semitism was deeply imbued not only in those who came to hate Jews but also in the victims. A good number of the Jews of Europe came to accept the message that they were, collectively, irredeemably different from the gentiles around them. This is what persistent and consistent forced isolation can do to you. And so the idea of difference, to the point that Jews could not live in the world except in a place set up for them alone (that is, a ghetto that they created and controlled) became part of the thought collective of those who sought their salvation in the ideology of Zionism. Israel, then, became a variant on the Russian and Polish shtetl.

That a long-term victim's thought collective should in some way come to be shaped by the persecutor's thought collective is not such an unusual proposition. But when this happens there is always the potential for a tragic twist. That is, in the fashion of the "battered child syndrome," the victim may well start to imitate the violent behavior of his persecutor. After all, the long-term victim is in many ways a product of the violence visited upon him and her. It is to be recalled that suffering does not build character, at least in the positive sense of the old saying. Rather it builds anger and resentment.

Palestine could not serve as the fulfillment of the ethnocentric demand that the Jews live in a place that is only for them—devoid of anyone who is different—as long as it was full of indigenous non-Jews. The Zionist thought collective came to be built, at least in good part, around the rationales that would allow the necessary ethnic cleansing to take place. Cultural genocide was a tactic pursued toward the end of ethnic cleansing. Thus we find within the thought collective of the Zionists the biblical mythology that asserts the existence of a divine deed to the land and, along with it, the transformation of the Palestinians into surrogate Nazis (or if you go with the Jewish Orthodox designation, Amalekites). In shaping their perceptions around this thought collective, the Israeli Jews, and Zionists in general, turned themselves into approximations of their own persecutors. They exchanged their identity as victims for a predatory identity. It is indeed an act of high tragedy.

Of course, the Palestinians too have their own thought collective, and after so many decades of Israeli persecution it also has been shaped by the worldview of the enemy. Zionists often point fingers at the Palestinians and call them anti-Semites. If this were completely true, the circular nature of these thought collectives would be complete: Russian anti-Semites produce Jewish persecutors who produce Palestinian anti-Semites. But the bulk of Palestinians appear to have, as yet, escaped this extreme consequence. This is perhaps because there is an active worldwide effort to support the struggle of the Palestinians, which includes non-Zionist Jews. This support may well have tempered the all-consuming anger that can often be found in the thought collectives of long-term victims.

Finally, in the case of Tibet we find one dominant thought collective—that of the Chinese People's Republic—displacing the indigenous, traditional thought collective of the Tibetan people. The question for the Chinese has always been, at what pace should this transformation take place? Slow or fast, the process surely amounts to cultural genocide. However, unlike Palestine, the aim here is not ethnic cleansing but rather assimilation.

To this end the Chinese have taken control of all the cultural organs of Tibet: the media, the arts, and most significantly the Tibetan Buddhist institutions of the country. These latter institutions, including the monasteries, temples, and Buddhist schools, were the backbone of traditional Tibetan culture. Under the Chinese they are purposefully being made devoid of meaning. There will then be nothing to stand in the way of the new thought collective rooted in Chinese ideology.

THE AMBIGUOUS LEGAL STATUS OF CULTURAL GENOCIDE

In the first chapter of this work it was noted that when, in December of 1948, the United Nations brought into formal being the Convention on the Prevention and Punishment of the Crime of Genocide, the act of cultural genocide was not included in the text. At the time there was a clear idea of what physical genocide was, for its unspeakable horror was fresh in the memories of all. But cultural genocide was apparently an amorphous notion to those composing the Genocide Convention. As a report of the Carnegie Council put it, "as the treaty was finalized a debate emerged over its proper scope. Many state representatives drafting the treaty understood cultural genocide to be analytically distinct, with one arguing forcefully that it defied both logic and proportion 'to include in the same convention both mass murders in gas chambers and the closing of libraries'" (Nersessian 2005).

As the two post-Holocaust examples of cultural genocide given in this work demonstrate, however, the modern manifestations of this phenomenon go well beyond the closing of libraries. Others have noticed this, too, and so cultural destruction has gained status as a marker of intent to commit genocide within the work of the International Criminal Tribunal for the Former Yugoslavia. It is recognized as a severe violation of rights in the Universal Declaration of Human Rights. Protection against cultural genocide is called for in the International Covenant on Economic, Social, and Cultural Rights, as well as in regional agreements such as the Charter of the European Union.

There is a qualitative difference between these instruments and the treaty on physical genocide, however. The latter can serve as the basis for criminal prosecution of individuals who perpetrate the act of genocide. The latter only holds states responsible and calls on these entities to stop cultural genocide and pay compensation. Yet states have no hard-and-fast existence apart from their citizens, bureaucracies, and leaders. If you cannot hold the human perpetrators responsible in a tangible way, you have no leverage against these acts.

The Carnegie Report states that cultural genocide should be brought under "customary international law. The need is patent. Cultural genocide is a unique wrong that should be recognized independently and that rises to the level of meriting individual criminal responsibility" (Narsessian 2005). Perhaps this will someday be achieved, but probably not soon, for the political will is not there.

The world has a short historical memory, and the years that have passed since the Holocaust have dulled recollection of the events that traumatized the West into creating the original genocide treaty. We are once more in a time cordial to double standards, a time when Western politicians seek to exempt themselves, their allies, and the powerful in general from the consequences of the most horrible of acts. Thus, if you are an African or Balkan or Muslim leader and commit genocidal acts you may well find yourself standing trial before the International Criminal Court. But if you are the leader of a great power or the favored ally of a great power you are now immune from such prosecution. This suggests a movement back to the time of imperialism, when Western nations slaughtered non-Westerners with impunity.

A good example of this trend is the present attack on the legal concept of universal jurisdiction. Universal jurisdiction is a legal process that allows private citizens resident in countries that are signatories to various international treaties such as the genocide convention and the Geneva conventions to institute prosecutions against alleged violators of the provisions of these treaties, even when these violations are committed outside the citizen's nation of residence. It is designed to prevent such alleged criminals from escaping justice by fleeing to a foreign place. In the wake of the Nazi Holocaust and other such crimes, universal jurisdiction was accepted as a necessary and positive legal step by almost all Western nations.

Now, as the years have passed and memories dimmed, there is a move to destroy universal jurisdiction because it can complicate diplomatic relations between states if one of those states has leaders or other notable citizens who could be charged under the treaties. These people are particularly vulnerable if it can be demonstrated that their home government has no intention of bringing them to trial for the alleged offenses.

A recent example of this is the effort on the part of private citizens in the United Kingdom to obtain warrants for the arrest of various Israeli civilian and military personnel visiting the country. These individuals, including the ex-foreign minister Tzipi Livini, are accused of war crimes in conjunction with Israel's January 2009 invasion of Gaza. The response of the British government was not to uphold its treaty obligations, but rather to attempt to undo the law so as not to be forced into a diplomatic confrontation with Israel.

THE PRESENT DILEMMA AND THE FUTURE OF
CULTURAL GENOCIDE

Our world still operates in a nation-state mode which holds high the principle of national sovereignty. The Holocaust was a soul-wrenching experience that warranted the partial reining in of that principle through the genocide convention and other international instruments. There are those who would dismiss these efforts as "quaint" and outmoded, and do away with them. We may think of our present dilemma in these terms: do we need regulation of our national or international behavior, or do we not? History would clearly suggest that we do. The entire history of diplomacy is a slow and imperfect record of establishment of rules and regulations. The history of the West immediately following World War II was a dramatic step forward in the process of necessary regulation of our national lives. Without these regulations we know that the world was, and would be again, a far more anarchistic place than it now is. And genocide is the very the pinnacle of that tendency toward anarchistic lawlessness.

The process of sensible regulation must be carried forward for all our sakes, not narrowed or even undone. The lesson of this work is that there are great roadblocks to moving forward, and natural localness is one of them. By extension, there are also the short-term outlooks of leaders and citizens trapped within their informational environments and thought collectives who would jeopardize the future to preserve the ethnocentric prejudices of the present moment.

Cultural genocide is alive and spreading in our world, and stands as a primary warning that if we do not break through the boundaries of our thought collectives we are doomed to reenact the wretched past, over and again. But it is doing so under the radar, so to speak, for there are no laws against it. And, as yet, it is not perceived to have reached the level of international scandal that makes for new laws and regulations. It would seem that such a scandal is what it would take for an event to break through the thought collectives of myriad cultures and peoples and get them to act collectively in their own interest. And even then, historical memory is all too brief.

BIBLIOGRAPHY

Anderson, B. 1991. *Imagined Communities.* New York: Verso.

Appadurai, A. 2006. *Fear of Small Numbers.* Durham: Duke University Press.

Atchison, B. 2011. "Rooms of Nicholas II—The New Study." http://alexanderpalace.org/palace/newstudy.html.

Ater, R. 1998. "Mental Health Issues of Resettled Refugees." http://ethnomed.org/clinical/mental-health/mental-health.

Al Jazeera. 2010. January 1. http://www.aljazeera.com/news/print.php?newid=328254.

BBC (British Broadcasting Corporation). 2009. "Row over Standard Hebrew Signs." July 13. http://news.bbc.co.uk/2/hi/middle_east/8148089.stm.

Berkowitz, B. 1999. "Information Age Intelligence." In *Domestic Sources of American Foreign Policy: Insights and Evidence,* ed. E. Wittkopf and J. McCormick, 207–211. 3rd ed. Lanham, Md.: Rowman and Littlefield.

Berman, S. 1997. *Children's Social Consciousness and the Development of Social Responsibility.* Albany: State University of New York Press.

Berry, W. 1990. "The Work of Local Culture." In *What Are People For?,* 153–169. San Francisco: North Point Press.

Cappon, L. 1959. *The Adams-Jefferson Letters.* Vol. 2. Chapel Hill: University of North Carolina Press.

Catlin, G. 1973. *Letters and Notes on the Manners, Customs, and Condition of the North American Indian.* Toronto: Dover Publications.

Chamberlain, K. 2005. "Stealing Palestinian History." *This Week in Palestine.* October. http://www.thisweekinpalestine.com/details.php?id=1451&ed=107&edid=107.

Chehata, H. 2010. "The Cultural Genocide of Palestine." *Middle East Monitor.*
    http://www.middleeastmonitor.org.uk/reports/by-dr-hanan-chehata/1061-
    the-cultural-genocide-of-palestine .

Chomsky, N., and E. Herman. 1988. *Manufacturing Consent: The Political
    Economy of the Mass Media.* New York: Pantheon.

Copeland, D. 1997. "Fighting for a Continent: Newspaper Coverage of the
    English and French War for Control of North America, 1754–1760." *Early
    American Review* (Spring). http://www.earlyamerica.com/review/spring97/
    newspapers.html.

Davidson, L. 2001. *America's Palestine: Popular and Official Perceptions from
    Balfour to Israeli Statehood.* Gainesville: University Press of Florida.

Dippie, B. 1982. *The Vanishing American: White Attitudes and U.S. Indian
    Policy.* Middletown: Wesleyan University Press.

Descartes, R. 2008. *Meditations on the First Philosophy.* Trans. John Veitch.
    New York: Cosimo.

Devlin, F. R. 2002. "Solzhenitsyn on the Jews and Tsarist Russia." *Occidental
    Quarterly* 8.4: 61–80.

Dostoevsky, F. [1877] 1995. "The Jews: Oppressed or Oppressors?" In *The Jew
    in the Modern World: A Documentary History,* ed. P. Mendes-Flohr and
    J. Reinharz, 337–339. 2nd ed. New York: Oxford University Press.

Dubnow, J. 1918. *The Jews in Russia and Poland.* Vol. 2. Philadelphia: Jewish
    Publication Society of America.

Edwards, D. 1982. "Nicholas I and Jewish Education." *History of Education
    Quarterly* 22.1 (Spring): 45–53.

Ehrman, B. 1999. *Jesus: Apocalyptic Prophet of the New Millennium.* New York:
    Oxford University Press.

Eldar, Akiva. 2003. "People and Politics/Sharon's Bantustans." *Haaretz.*
    May 13. http://www.haaretz.com/print-edition/features/people-and-politics-
    sharon-s-bantustans-are-far-from-copenhagen-s-hope-1.10275.

Ericson, E., and D. Mahoney, eds. 2006. *The Solzhenitsyn Reader: New and
    Essential Writings 1947–2005.* Wilmington, Del.: ISI Books.

Fleck, L. 1979. *The Genesis and Development of a Scientific Fact.* Chicago:
    University of Chicago Press.

Frankl, O. 1949. *Theodor Herzl, the Jew and the Man: A Portrait.* New York:
    Storm.

Gellner, E. 1992. *Reason and Culture.* Cambridge, Mass.: Blackwell.

Ghanem, A. 2001. *The Palestinian-Arab Minority in Israel, 1948–2000.* Albany:
    State University of New York Press.

Gonzalez, M., C. Hidalgo, and A. Barabasi. 2008. "Understanding Individual Mobility Patterns." *Nature* 453 (June): 779–782.

Gourevitch, P. 1998. *We Wish to Inform You That Tomorrow We Will Be Killed with Our Families.* New York: Farrar, Strauss and Giroux.

Granitsas, A. 2005. "Americans Are Tuning Out the World." *Yale Global On Line.* November 24. http://yaleglobal.yale.edu/content/americans-are-tuning-out-world.

Haas, E. 2000. *Nationalism, Liberalism, and Progress.* Vol. 2. Ithaca: Cornell University Press.

Harcave, S. 2004. *Count Sergei Witte and the Twilight of Imperial Russia.* New York: M. E. Sharpe.

Heuer, M. 1999. "Group Blasts Destruction of Palestinian Culture." *JTA.* November 30. http://www.jta.org/news/article/1999/11/30/9075/library groupthrows.

Hunt, M. 1987. *Ideology and U.S. Foreign Policy.* New Haven: Yale University Press.

Huntington, S. 1996. *The Clash of Civilizations and the Remaking of World Order.* New York: Simon and Schuster.

"The Internet Study: More Detail." 2000. Stanford University Institute for the Quantitative Study of Society. February. http://www.scribd.com/doc/12819360/internet-usage.

Janis, I. 1972. *Victims of Groupthink.* Atlanta: Houghton Mifflin.

Jerusalem Post. 2000. August 30.

Jewish Virtual Library. 2010. "Union of the Russian People." http://www.jewishvirtuallibrary.org/jsource/judaica/ejud_0002_0020_0_20205.html.

Jewish Virtual Library. 2011a. "Jewish Virtual History Tour." February Revolution, Nicholas II. http://www.jewishvirtuallibrary.org/jsource/vjw/russia.html.

Jewish Virtual Library. 2011b. "Jewish Virtual History Tour." Nicholas I. http://www.jewishvirtuallibrary.org/jsource/vjw/russia.html#d.

Johnson, P. 1987. *A History of the Jews.* New York: Harper and Row.

Joseph, S. 1914. "Jewish Immigration to the U.S. from 1881 to 1910." Ph.D. dissertation, Columbia University.

Kawashima, Y. 1986. *Puritan Justice and the Indian.* Middletown: Wesleyan University Press.

Kletter, R. 2005. *Just Past? The Making of Israeli Archeology.* London: Equinox.

Kniesmeyer, J., and D. Brecher. 1995. "Beyond the Pale, Jews in the Russian Empire, Alexander II—A Brief Spring." http://www.friends-partners.org/ partners/beyond-the-pale/english/32.html.

Laird, T. 2006. *The Story of Tibet: Conversations with the Dalai Lama.* New York: Grove.

Lamroza, J., and S. Klier. 1998. *Pogroms: Anti-Jewish Violence in Modern Russian History.* Cambridge: Cambridge University Press.

Larson, S. 1997. "Fear and Contempt: A European Concept of Property." *American Indian Quarterly* 21.4 (Fall): 567–577.

Layman, M. 1942. "A History of Indian Education in the United States." Ph.D. dissertation, University of Minnesota.

Leacock, E., ed. 1963. *Lewis Henry Morgan, Ancient Society or Research in the Lines of Human Progress from Savagery through Barbarism to Civilization.* Burtonsville, Md.: Meridian Books.

Lilenthal, A. 1979. *The Zionist Connection, What Price Peace?* New York: Middle East Perspective.

Lippman, W. [1922] 1997. *Public Opinion.* New York: Free Press Paperbacks.

Lis, J., and J. Khoury. 2009. "Police Disperse Palestinian Cultural Festival Events." *Haaretz.* April 4. http://www.haaretz.com/news/police-disperse-palestinian-culture-festival-events-1.272577.

Madariaqa, I. de. 2002. *Catherine the Great: A Short History.* New Haven: Yale University Press.

Masalha, N. 1992. *Expulsion of the Palestinians: The Concept of Transfer in Zionist Political Thought, 1882–1948.* Washington, D.C.: Institute for Palestine Studies.

McLoughlin, W. G. 1984. *Cherokees and Missionaries.* New Haven: Yale University Press.

McLuhan, M. 1964. *Understanding Media.* New York: Mentor.

———. 1967. *The Medium Is the Message.* New York: Bantam.

Meehan, M. 1999. "Israeli Textbooks and Children's Literature Promote Racism and Hatred toward Palestinians and Arabs." *Washington Report on Middle East Affairs*, September, 19–20.

Mohr, W. 1933. *Federal Indian Relations 1774–1788.* Philadelphia: University of Pennsylvania Press.

Morgan, L. H. 1877. *Ancient Societies: Researches in the Lines of Human Progress from Savagery, through Barbarism, to Civilization.* http://www.deleonism.org/lewis-henry-morgan-ancient-society.htm.

Morris, B. 1987. *The Birth of the Palestinian Refugee Problem 1947–1949.* New York: Cambridge University Press.

———. 1999. *Righteous Victims: A History of the Zionist-Arab Conflict 1881–1999.* New York: Alfred A. Knopf.

Morse, J. 1822. *A Report to the Secretary of War of the U.S. on Indian Affairs.* New Haven, Conn.: S. Converse.

Mueller, J. 1999. "Public Opinion and Foreign Policy: The People's Common Sense." In *Domestic Sources of American Foreign Policy: Insights and Evidence,* ed. E. Wittkopf and J. McCormick, 50–61. 3rd ed. Lanham, Md.: Rowman and Littlefield.

Nash, G. 1974. *Red, White, and Black: The Peoples of Early America.* Englewood Cliffs, N.J.: Prentice Hall.

Nersessian, D. April 22, 2005. "Rethinking Cultural Genocide under International Law." Carnegie Council. http://www.carnegiecouncil.org/resources/publications/dialogue/2_12/section_1/5139.html.

Ngai, M. 2004. *Impossible Subjects: Illegal Aliens and the Making of Modern America.* Princeton: Princeton University Press.

Oatley, K. 2004. *Emotions: A Brief History.* New York: Free Press.

Palestine Monitor. 2009. "The Power of Culture vs the Culture of Power." June 5. http://www.palestinemonitor.org/spip/spip.php?article974.

Palomino, M. 1971. "Blood Libels against Jews in Modern Russia, 1799 to after 1948." *Encyclopedia Judaica:* 4. http://www.geschichteinchronologie.ch/russland-bis-1917/EncJud_ansiedlungsrayon03b-blutverleumdungen-1799-nach1948-ENGL.html.

Pappe, I. 2004. *A History of Modern Palestine: One Land, Two Peoples.* Cambridge: Cambridge University Press.

———. 2007. *The Ethnic Cleansing of Palestine.* Oxford: Oneworld Publications.

Perlmann, M. 1981. "The British Embassy in St. Petersburg on Russian Jewry." *Proceeding of the American Academy of Jewish Research* 48: 297–308.

Philbrick, N. 2006. *Mayflower.* New York: Viking Press.

Pinker, S. 1997. *How the Mind Works.* New York: Norton.

Pitt, W. 2007. "Dan Rather's Magnum Opus." *Truthout.* September 26. http://lists.fahamu.org/pipermail/debate-list/2007-September/007787.html.

Posner, R. 2003. *Law, Pragmatism. and Democracy.* Cambridge: Harvard University Press.

Prucha, F. 1984. *The Great Father: The U.S. Government and the American Indians.* Lincoln: University of Nebraska Press.

Puglisi, M. 1991. "Capt. John Smith, Pocahontas, and a Clash of Cultures: A Case of Ethnohistorical Perspective." *History Teacher* 25.1: 97–103.

Radziwill, C. 1931. *Nicolas II, the Last of the Tsars.* London: Cassell.

Rapoport, M. 2008. "Special Document: History Erased, the IDF and the Post-1948 Destruction of Palestinian Monuments." *Journal of Palestine Studies* 2 (Winter): 82–88.

Ravenal, E. 1978. *Never Again: Learning from America's Foreign Policy Failures.* Philadelphia: Temple University Press.

Reyhner, J., and J. Eder. 2004. *American Indian Education: A History.* Norman: University of Oklahoma Press.

Riasanovsky, N. 1959. *Nicholas I and Official Nationality in Russia, 1825–1855.* Berkeley: University of California Press.

———. 2000. *A History of Russia.* New York: Oxford University Press.

Roehm, M. 1966. *The Letters of George Catlin and His Family: A Chronicle of the American West.* Berkeley: University of California Press.

Rosenthal, H. 2002. "Catherine II." Jewish Encyclopedia.com. http://www .jewishencyclopedia.com/view.jsp?artid=275&letter=C.

Roundtree, H. 1996. *Pocahontas's People: The Powhatan Indians of Virginia through the Ages.* Norman: University of Oklahoma Press.

Russian History Encyclopedia. 2004. http://www.answers.com/topic/censorship #Gale_Encyclopedia_of_Russian_History_d.

Sajed, A. N.d. "Boundaries." *Globalization and Autonomy Online Compendium.* http://www.globalautonomy.ca/global1/glossary_entry.jsp?id=C0.0060.

Shakya, T. 1999. *The Dragon in the Land of Snows.* New York: Penguin Compass.

Shamir, Y. 1988. *New York Times.* April 1. http://query.nytimes.com/gst/ fullpage.html?res=940DE1DD1F3DF932A35757C0A96E948260.

Shenkman, R. 2008. *Just How Stupid Are We? Facing the Truth about the American Voter.* New York: Basic Books.

Shmulevich, A., and M. Kipnis. 2005. "Judaisers." *Notes of Jewish History* 1.50 (January): 635–638.

Simons, C. 2003. "An Historical Survey of Proposals to Transfer Arabs from Palestine, 1895–1947." Subsections on Chaim Weizmann and David Ben Gurion. http://www.chaimsimons.net/transfer.html.

Smith, C. 1988. *Palestine and the Arab-Israeli Conflict.* New York: St. Martin's.

"Statutes Concerning the Organization of the Jews." 1804. December 9. http://www.ldorvdor.net/laws.html.

Strobel, W. 1999. "The CNN Effect: Myth or Reality?" In *Domestic Sources of American Foreign Policy: Insights and Evidence*, ed. E. Wittkopf and J. McCormick, 85–94. 3rd ed. Lanham, Md.: Rowman and Littlefield.

Surowiecki, J. 2005. *The Wisdom of Crowds*. New York: Anchor Books.

Terry, J. 2005. *U.S. Foreign Policy in the Middle East: The Role of Lobbies and Special Interest Groups*. London: Pluto.

Tessler, M. 1994. *A History of the Arab-Israeli Conflict*. Bloomington: Indiana University Press.

Thorton, R. 1990. *American Indian Holocaust and Survival*. Norman: University of Oklahoma Press.

Tinker, G. 1993. *Missionary Conquest: The Gospel and Native American Cultural Genocide*. Minneapolis: Fortress.

Vaughn, A. T. 1978. "Expulsion of the Savages, English Policy and the Virginia Massacre of 1622." *William and Mary Quarterly* 35.1: 57–84.

Wang, L. and T. Shakya. 2009. *The Struggle for Tibet*. London: Verso.

Warth, R. 1997. *Nicholas II: The Life and Reign of Russia's Last Monarch*. Santa Barbara, Cal.: Praeger.

Weinberg, A. 1963. *Manifest Destiny*. [1935] reprint Chicago: Quadrangle Books.

Weizmann, C. 1942. "Palestine's Role in the Solution of the Jewish Problem." *Foreign Affairs* 20.2: 324–338.

———. 1983. *The Letters and Papers* (Series B, Vol. 1). Piscataway, N.J.: Transaction.

Willingham, D. 2007. "Critical Thinking: Why It Is So Hard to Teach." *American Educator* (Summer): 8–19.

Witte, S. 1990. *The Memoirs of Count Witte*. Armonk, N.Y.: M. E. Sharpe. Online at http://euphrates.wpunj.edu/courses/hist330-60/Supplementary%20Material/HTML/October%20Manifesto.html.

Wittkopf, E., and J. McCormack, eds. 1999. *Domestic Sources of American Foreign Policy: Insights and Evidence*. 3rd ed. Lanham, Md.: Rowman and Littlefield.

Zohn, H., trans. 1960. *The Complete Diaries of Theodor Herzl*. Vol. 1. New York: Herzl Press.

INDEX

Abdullah, emir (later king) of Jordan, 71, 76
Adams, John, 28
affiliation, 9
aggression, toward out-groups, 5. *See also* assertiveness
Al Aqsa Mosque, 81–82
Alexander I, czar, 49–52
Alexander II, czar, 54–56
Alexander III, czar, 57–59
aliens, "illegal," 6. *See also* "other"
Amalekites, Palestinians as, 126
Amban (Chinese residential commissioner), role of in Tibet, 91–92
American Library Association, 81
American Revolution, and Indians, 30, 31
Anderson, Benedict, 5, 9, 87
Anglo-Powhatan War, 24
anti-Palestinian political parties, 86
anti-Semitism, European, 125; Nazi, 67. *See also* anti-Semitism, Russian; the Holocaust
anti-Semitism, Russian: grassroots, 44–48, 55, 64, 114, 115, 124; in late-empire politics, 85; in mass media, 49; and the 1905 revolution, 62–63; in novels, 55–57; during reign of Catherine the Great, 48; as state policy, 46. *See also*

anti-Semitism, European; the Holocaust
Appadurai, Arjun, 13, 48, 63, 114
Arab Education Committee in Support of Local Councils, 79–80
archaeologists, Israeli: lied to about destruction of holy sites, 79; and the undermining of Al Aqsa Mosque, 81
army service, in Israel, Palestinians shut out from benefits of, 83
Ashkenazi Jews, in Palestine, 74
assertiveness, 8–9. *See also* aggression
assimilation: absent from Israeli policy toward Palestinians, 86; of American Indians, 29, 42; as Chinese policy toward Tibetans, 127; as goal of CCP for Tibetans, 110; of Jews into Western society, 66; lack of, among Russian Jews, 45; of minorities, as Russian state policy, 53; "Russianization" of Jews, 50, 51, 53
Atamneh, Jamal, 79–80
attachment, 9

Balfour Declaration, 69, 116
Bantustan model, 85
Barak, Ehud, 85
Barakeh, Mohammad, 82
Barbour, James, 35
Bar-Tal, Daniel, 79

ABOUT THE AUTHOR

LAWRENCE DAVIDSON is a professor of history at West Chester University in West Chester, Pennsylvania. His specialization is the history of American relations with the Middle East. He is the author of five previous books and numerous articles. Professor Davidson maintains a blog that can be found at www.tothepointanalyses.com.

CPSIA information can be obtained at www.ICGtesting.com
Printed in the USA
BVOW071626300112

281667BV00002B/1/P